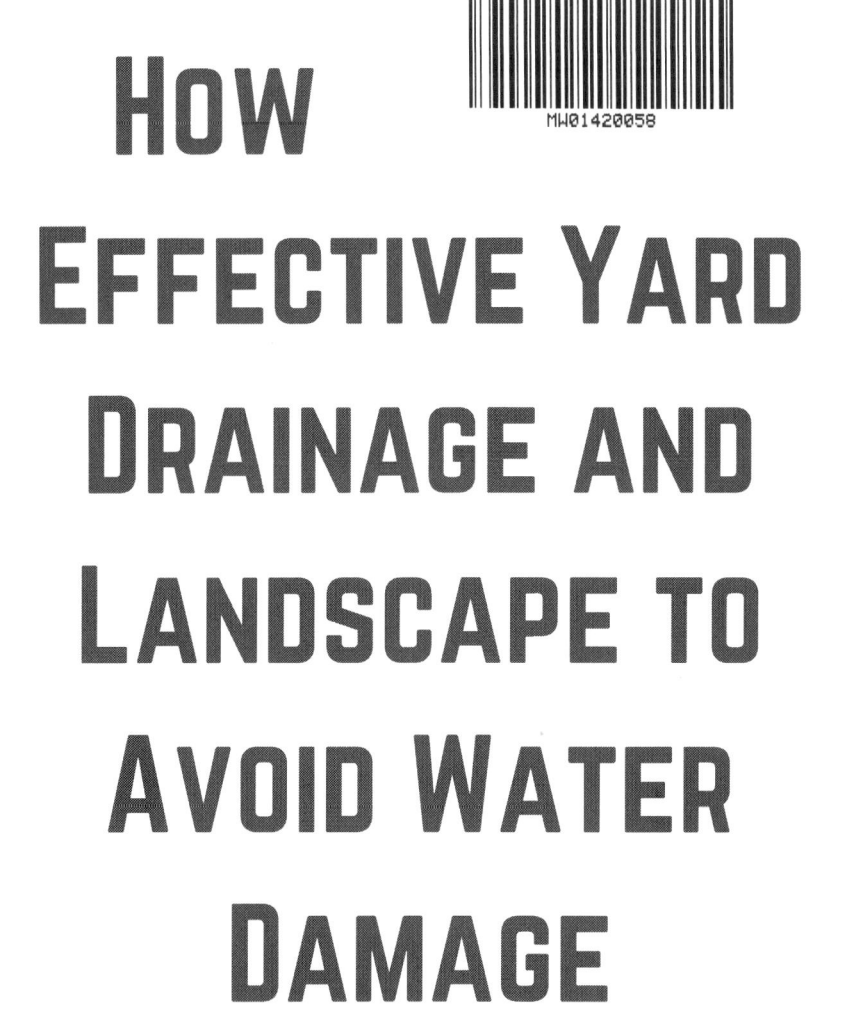

How Effective Yard Drainage and Landscape to Avoid Water Damage

The Ultimate Guide to Yard Drainage Solutions, Landscape Grading Techniques, and Water Damage Prevention: Expert Tips for Homeowners, Gardeners, and Landscapers

The Fix It Guy

Copyright © 2024 by The Fix It Guy

All rights reserved. No part of this book may be reproduced in any form or by any electronic or mechanical means, including information storage and retrieval systems, without permission in writing from the publisher, except by a reviewer who may quote brief passages in a review.

Table of Contents

Introduction

Chapter 1: Understanding Yard Drainage Basics
- Types of Soil and Their Impact on Drainage
- Identifying Problem Areas in Your Yard
- The Role of Topography and Slope in Yard Drainage
- Calculating Runoff and Drainage Capacity

Chapter 2: Drainage Solutions for Your Yard
- Surface Drainage Techniques
    - Grading and Contouring
    - Swales and Berms
    - French Drains and Trench Drains
    - Catch Basins and Grates
- Subsurface Drainage Methods
    - Perforated Pipes and Drainage Tiles
    - Dry Wells and Soakaways
    - Sump Pumps and Lift Stations
- Choosing the Right Drainage Solution for Your Yard

Chapter 3: Landscaping Techniques for Improved Drainage
- Rain Gardens and Bioswales
- Permeable Pavers and Porous Surfaces
- Terracing and Retaining Walls
- Planting Strategies for Better Drainage
- Maintaining Your Drainage-Friendly Landscape

Chapter 4: Preventing Water Damage in Your Home
- Gutter and Downspout Maintenance
- Foundation Waterproofing and Grading

- Sump Pump Installation and Maintenance
- Identifying and Fixing Leaks and Moisture Issues

Chapter 5: DIY Drainage Projects and Maintenance
- Tools and Materials for Yard Drainage Projects
- Step-by-Step Guides for Common Drainage Installations
- Maintenance Checklist for Drainage Systems
- Troubleshooting Common Drainage Problems

Chapter 6: Case Studies and Success Stories
- Real-Life Examples of Effective Yard Drainage Solutions
- Before and After Transformations
- Lessons Learned from Homeowners and Professionals

Conclusion

Introduction

Picture this: you're standing in your backyard, admiring the lush green grass, the vibrant flowerbeds, and the stunning landscaping you've worked so hard to create. But then, you notice a problem. Puddles of water are forming in low-lying areas, and the soil is becoming saturated and spongy. You realize that your yard's drainage issues are not only damaging your landscape but also threatening the foundation of your home.

If this scenario sounds all too familiar, you're not alone. As a homeowner, gardener, or landscaper, you know that proper yard drainage and landscaping are essential for maintaining a beautiful and healthy outdoor space. But what you might not know is that poor drainage can lead to a host of problems, from unsightly water damage to costly foundation repairs.

That's where "How to Plan Effective Yard Drainage and Landscape to Avoid Water Damage" comes in. This ultimate guide is your key to unlocking the secrets of yard drainage solutions, landscape grading techniques, and water damage prevention. With expert tips tailored specifically for homeowners, gardeners, and landscapers like you, this book will empower you to take control of your yard's drainage and protect your home from the devastating effects of water damage.

But why is proper yard drainage and landscaping so important? Well, let me tell you a story. When I first bought my home, I was excited to create the backyard oasis of my dreams.

I spent countless hours planting, mulching, and designing the perfect landscape. But after just one heavy rainstorm, I watched in horror as my hard work was washed away by a river of water that had nowhere else to go.

That's when I realized that I had neglected one of the most critical aspects of yard maintenance: drainage. I had fallen victim to one of the most common causes of water damage in yards and landscapes – poor grading and inadequate drainage solutions. And I knew I had to do something about it.

Through extensive research and countless hours of trial and error, I discovered the benefits of implementing effective drainage solutions. Not only did proper drainage protect my landscape from water damage, but it also improved the health of my plants, prevented soil erosion, and even increased the value of my home.

In this book, I'll share with you everything I've learned about yard drainage and landscaping. From understanding the basics of soil types and topography to choosing the right drainage solutions for your specific needs, you'll gain the knowledge and skills necessary to create a yard that is both beautiful and functional.

But this book isn't just about theory – it's about practical, actionable advice that you can implement right away. With step-by-step guides, real-life case studies, and a wealth of resources at your fingertips, you'll have everything you need to tackle even the most challenging drainage projects with confidence.

So whether you're a seasoned landscaper looking to expand your expertise or a homeowner desperate to save your yard from the ravages of water damage, this book is for you. Don't let poor drainage rob you of the outdoor oasis you've always dreamed of. Take control of your yard's health and beauty with "How to Plan Effective Yard Drainage and Landscape to Avoid Water Damage – The Ultimate Guide to Yard Drainage Solutions, Landscape Grading Techniques, and Water Damage Prevention: Expert Tips for Homeowners, Gardeners, and Landscapers."

Chapter 1
Understanding Yard Drainage Basics
Types of Soil and Their Impact on Drainage

Understanding the type of soil in your yard is crucial for planning effective drainage solutions. Different soil types have varying characteristics that influence how water moves through them, affecting the overall drainage of your landscape. In this section, we'll explore the main types of soil and their impact on yard drainage.

Sandy Soil
 a. Characteristics
  - Large, coarse particles with ample space between them
  - High porosity and permeability
  - Excellent drainage properties
  - Low water and nutrient retention capacity
 b. Impact on Drainage
  - Water moves quickly through sandy soil, reducing the risk of waterlogging
  - Ideal for areas with high rainfall or poor drainage
  - May require more frequent irrigation due to low water retention
 c. Improving Sandy Soil for Better Drainage
   - Incorporate organic matter to improve water and nutrient retention
   - Use mulch to reduce evaporation and maintain soil moisture
   - Consider installing a drip irrigation system for efficient watering

Clay Soil
a. Characteristics
- Small, fine particles with limited space between them
- Low porosity and permeability
- Poor drainage properties
- High water and nutrient retention capacity

b. Impact on Drainage
- Water moves slowly through clay soil, increasing the risk of waterlogging
- Prone to compaction, further reducing drainage capabilities
- Can lead to root rot and other plant health issues

c. Improving Clay Soil for Better Drainage
- Amend soil with organic matter, such as compost or aged manure
- Incorporate sand or gypsum to improve soil structure and drainage
- Install subsurface drainage systems, like French drains or drainage tiles
- Avoid working with clay soil when it's wet to prevent compaction

Loamy Soil
a. Characteristics
- A balanced mixture of sand, silt, and clay particles
- Moderate porosity and permeability
- Good drainage properties
- Adequate water and nutrient retention capacity

b. Impact on Drainage
- Water moves at a moderate rate through loamy soil, providing optimal drainage

- Ideal for most plants, as it offers a balance of drainage and moisture retention
- Supports healthy root growth and plant development

c. Maintaining Loamy Soil for Optimal Drainage
- Regularly incorporate organic matter to maintain soil structure and fertility
- Avoid overworking the soil to prevent compaction
- Use mulch to protect soil surface and regulate soil temperature and moisture

Silty Soil

a. Characteristics
- Medium-sized particles, smaller than sand but larger than clay
- Moderate porosity and permeability
- Fair to poor drainage properties
- Moderate water and nutrient retention capacity

b. Impact on Drainage
- Water moves moderately through silty soil, but drainage can be slow
- Prone to compaction, which can further impede drainage
- Can lead to waterlogging and poor plant growth in heavy rainfall areas

c. Improving Silty Soil for Better Drainage
- Incorporate organic matter to improve soil structure and drainage
- Avoid overwatering and allow soil to dry between watering sessions
- Use raised beds or mounds to improve drainage in problematic areas

Determining Your Soil Type
 a. Visual Assessment
 - Observe soil color, texture, and consistency
 - Note how quickly water drains after rainfall or irrigation
 b. Soil Texture Test
 - Take a small amount of moist soil and roll it between your hands
 - Evaluate soil texture based on its ability to form a ribbon or ball
 c. Professional Soil Analysis
 - Collect soil samples from different parts of your yard
 - Send samples to a local cooperative extension office or soil testing lab
 - Receive a detailed report on soil type, pH, nutrient levels, and drainage properties

By understanding the types of soil present in your yard and their impact on drainage, you can make informed decisions when planning and implementing drainage solutions. In the following sections, we'll explore how to identify problem areas in your yard, assess topography and slope, and calculate runoff and drainage capacity to create a comprehensive drainage plan tailored to your specific needs.

Identifying Problem Areas in Your Yard

Before you can implement effective drainage solutions, it's essential to identify the problem areas in your yard. By conducting a thorough assessment of your landscape, you can pinpoint the specific locations where water tends to accumulate or where drainage issues are causing damage to your plants, lawn, or home's foundation. In this section, we'll discuss how to identify problem areas and what signs to look for.

Visual Inspection
 a. Observe Your Yard After Rain or Irrigation
- Take note of areas where water puddles or pools for an extended period
- Look for signs of soil erosion, such as gullies or washed-out areas
- Identify low-lying areas where water naturally collects

 b. Check for Soggy or Spongy Soil
- Walk through your yard and feel for areas where the soil remains soggy or spongy long after rain or irrigation
- These areas may indicate poor drainage or a high water table

 c. Inspect Plant Health
- Look for plants that show signs of stress, such as yellowing leaves, wilting, or stunted growth
- Poor drainage can lead to root rot and other plant health issues

 d. Examine Hardscapes and Structures
- Check for signs of water damage on patios, walkways, or retaining walls

- Look for cracks in the foundation or water stains on basement walls, which may indicate drainage problems

Slope and Grading Assessment
a. Observe Water Flow Direction
- During a rainstorm or when running a hose, observe the direction of water flow in your yard
- Identify areas where water is flowing towards your home's foundation or other structures

b. Check for Proper Grading
- Ensure that the soil around your home's foundation slopes away from the structure at a rate of 6 inches for every 10 feet
- Look for areas where the grading is flat or slopes towards the foundation

c. Assess Slope Severity
- Identify areas with steep slopes that may contribute to rapid water runoff and soil erosion
- Determine if the slope severity is causing drainage issues or making it difficult to maintain plant growth

Gutter and Downspout Evaluation
a. Check for Proper Gutter Installation
- Ensure that gutters are properly secured to the roofline and have a slight slope towards the downspouts
- Look for sagging, leaking, or overflowing gutters that may contribute to drainage problems

b. Assess Downspout Placement
- Check that downspouts are directing water away from your home's foundation and not contributing to pooling or soggy areas in your yard

- Ensure that downspouts extend at least 4 feet away from the foundation or are connected to a drainage system

c. Identify Clogged Gutters and Downspouts
- Remove debris, such as leaves and twigs, that may be clogging gutters and downspouts
- Clogged gutters can cause water to overflow and contribute to drainage issues

Soil Compaction Assessment

a. Perform a Screwdriver Test
- Push a screwdriver or similar tool into the soil in various locations throughout your yard
- If the screwdriver is difficult to push in or meets resistance, the soil may be compacted

b. Observe Water Infiltration
- After rain or irrigation, observe how quickly water is absorbed into the soil
- Slow water infiltration may indicate soil compaction, which can hinder drainage

c. Evaluate Foot Traffic and Heavy Equipment Use
- Identify areas where frequent foot traffic or the use of heavy equipment may have contributed to soil compaction
- Compacted soil can prevent water from properly draining and lead to pooling or runoff

Professional Drainage Assessment

a. Consult with a Landscape Professional
- If you're unsure about the severity of your drainage issues or need guidance on identifying problem areas, consider hiring a landscape professional

- A professional can conduct a thorough assessment of your yard's drainage and provide recommendations for improvement

b. Request a Drainage Plan
- Ask the landscape professional to create a detailed drainage plan that addresses the specific issues in your yard
- The plan should include recommendations for grading, slope adjustment, and the installation of appropriate drainage solutions

By carefully identifying the problem areas in your yard, you can develop a targeted approach to improving drainage and preventing water damage. In the next section, we'll explore how topography and slope play a crucial role in yard drainage and how to assess these factors to create a comprehensive drainage plan.

The Role of Topography and Slope in Yard Drainage

Topography and slope play a crucial role in how water moves through your yard and how effectively it drains. Understanding the interplay between these factors and your yard's drainage can help you make informed decisions when planning and implementing drainage solutions. In this section, we'll explore the importance of topography and slope in yard drainage and how to assess these factors to create a comprehensive drainage plan.

Topography
  a. Definition
- Topography refers to the physical features and contours of your yard's surface
- It includes natural elements such as hills, valleys, and flat areas

  b. Impact on Drainage
- Topography determines the direction and speed of water flow in your yard
- Water naturally flows from higher elevations to lower elevations due to gravity
- Low-lying areas, depressions, and flat surfaces are more prone to water accumulation and poor drainage

  c. Assessing Your Yard's Topography
- Observe the natural contours and features of your yard
- Identify high points, low points, and any areas where water naturally collects
- Use a topographic map or hire a professional to create a detailed survey of your yard's topography

Slope
a. Definition
- Slope refers to the degree of incline or steepness of your yard's surface
- It is typically measured as a percentage or ratio, such as a 2% slope or a 1:50 slope

b. Impact on Drainage
- The slope of your yard greatly influences how quickly water moves across the surface and how well it drains
- A gentle slope (1-2%) allows water to slowly flow away from structures and infiltrate into the soil
- A steep slope (>5%) can cause water to move too quickly, leading to soil erosion and reduced infiltration
- Flat or level areas (<1% slope) may have poor drainage and be prone to water accumulation

c. Assessing Your Yard's Slope
- Use a level and measuring tape to determine the slope in various areas of your yard
- Place the level horizontally on the ground and measure the vertical distance between the ground and the end of the level
- Divide the vertical distance by the horizontal distance (length of the level) and multiply by 100 to calculate the slope percentage

Ideal Slope for Proper Drainage
a. Recommended Slope Range
- A slope between 1-2% is ideal for proper drainage in most yard situations
- This gentle slope allows water to move away from structures and into drainage systems or permeable surfaces

b. Slope Around Foundations
- The soil around your home's foundation should slope away from the structure at a rate of 6 inches for every 10 feet (5% slope)
- This slope helps prevent water from pooling near the foundation and potentially causing damage

c. Sloped Yard Challenges and Solutions
- Steep slopes can make it difficult to maintain plant growth and can contribute to soil erosion
- Terracing, retaining walls, and proper plant selection can help stabilize steep slopes and improve drainage
- Flat areas may require the installation of French drains, catch basins, or other subsurface drainage solutions to prevent water accumulation

Modifying Topography and Slope for Improved Drainage

a. Grading
- Grading involves altering the contours of your yard's surface to direct water flow away from structures and into appropriate drainage areas
- Cut and fill techniques are used to remove soil from high points and add it to low points, creating a more even slope

b. Swales and Berms
- Swales are shallow, linear depressions that are designed to channel water flow and promote infiltration
- Berms are raised mounds of soil that can be used to direct water flow and create barriers to prevent water from reaching certain areas

c. Professional Landscape Assistance
- If significant modifications to your yard's topography or slope are needed, consider hiring a landscape professional
- A professional can assess your yard's specific needs, develop a grading plan, and ensure that modifications are made correctly and safely

By understanding the role of topography and slope in yard drainage, you can better assess your yard's unique characteristics and develop a tailored approach to improving drainage. In the next section, we'll discuss how to calculate runoff and drainage capacity to ensure that your chosen drainage solutions are adequately sized and effective.

Calculating Runoff and Drainage Capacity

Calculating runoff and drainage capacity is essential for designing and implementing effective drainage solutions in your yard. Runoff refers to the portion of rainfall or irrigation water that does not infiltrate into the soil and instead flows across the surface. Drainage capacity is the ability of your yard's drainage system to handle and manage this runoff. In this section, we'll explore how to calculate runoff and drainage capacity to ensure that your chosen drainage solutions are adequately sized and effective.

Factors Affecting Runoff

  a. Rainfall Intensity and Duration
- The amount and intensity of rainfall directly influence the volume of runoff generated
- More intense rainfall events produce higher runoff rates and volumes

  b. Soil Type and Infiltration Rate
- The type of soil in your yard affects how quickly water can infiltrate into the ground
- Sandy soils have higher infiltration rates, while clay soils have lower infiltration rates, leading to increased runoff

  c. Land Cover and Vegetation
- The presence of vegetation, such as grass, trees, and shrubs, can slow down runoff and increase infiltration
- Impervious surfaces, like pavement and roofs, prevent infiltration and generate higher runoff volumes

d. Slope and Topography
- Steeper slopes and complex topography can contribute to increased runoff velocity and volume
- Flatter areas may have slower runoff rates but can be prone to water accumulation if drainage is poor

Calculating Runoff Volume
a. Rational Method
- The Rational Method is a simple approach to estimating peak runoff rates for small drainage areas
- The formula is: $Q = C \times I \times A$, where:
- Q is the peak runoff rate in cubic feet per second (cfs)
- C is the runoff coefficient, which depends on land cover and soil type (ranges from 0.1 to 1.0)
- I is the rainfall intensity in inches per hour for a specific duration and return period
- A is the drainage area in acres

b. SCS Curve Number Method
- The SCS Curve Number Method, developed by the USDA Soil Conservation Service (now NRCS), estimates runoff volume based on soil type, land use, and antecedent moisture conditions
- The method uses a curve number (CN) to represent the runoff potential of a specific area
- Higher CNs indicate greater runoff potential, while lower CNs indicate more infiltration and less runoff
- Runoff volume is calculated using rainfall depth and the CN value

c. Online Calculators and Tools
- Various online calculators and tools are available to help estimate runoff volume based on specific site conditions
- These tools often require inputs such as location, soil type, land cover, and rainfall data
- Examples include the EPA's National Stormwater Calculator and the Green Values Stormwater Management Calculator

Drainage Capacity and Sizing
a. Determine Required Capacity
- Once runoff volume is calculated, the required drainage capacity can be determined
- Drainage capacity should be sized to handle the expected runoff volume from a design storm event (e.g., a 10-year, 24-hour storm)
- The design storm event is selected based on local regulations and the level of protection desired

b. Sizing Drainage Components
- Drainage components, such as pipes, culverts, and catch basins, should be sized to accommodate the required drainage capacity
- Pipe size is determined by considering factors such as slope, roughness, and allowable flow velocity
- Catch basins and inlets should be sized and spaced appropriately to efficiently capture and convey runoff

c. Professional Assistance
- Calculating runoff and sizing drainage components can be complex, especially for larger or more complex sites
- Consider hiring a professional engineer or landscape architect to perform the necessary calculations and design a suitable drainage system

Incorporating Sustainable Drainage Practices
a. Low Impact Development (LID)
- LID practices aim to mimic natural drainage patterns and promote infiltration and evapotranspiration
- Examples include rain gardens, bioswales, permeable pavers, and green roofs
- These practices can reduce runoff volume and improve water quality

b. Rainwater Harvesting
- Collecting and storing rainwater from roofs and other surfaces can reduce runoff and provide a valuable water resource for irrigation
- Rain barrels and cisterns are common rainwater harvesting methods

c. Soil Amendments and Vegetation
- Improving soil structure and fertility through the use of organic amendments can increase infiltration and reduce runoff
- Planting deep-rooted vegetation and maintaining a healthy lawn can also help to slow down runoff and promote infiltration

By understanding how to calculate runoff and drainage capacity, you can ensure that your yard's drainage solutions are properly sized and effective. Incorporating sustainable drainage practices can further enhance the performance of your drainage system while providing additional environmental benefits. In the next chapter, we'll explore specific drainage solutions and how to choose the right options for your yard's unique needs.

Chapter 2
Drainage Solutions for Your Yard
Surface Drainage Techniques
Grading and Contouring

Surface drainage techniques are designed to manage water runoff and prevent water accumulation on the surface of your yard. These techniques involve altering the shape and contours of the land to direct water flow away from structures and into appropriate drainage areas. In this section, we'll explore various surface drainage techniques, with a focus on grading and contouring.

Grading and Contouring
  a. Definition
- Grading is the process of reshaping the surface of your yard to create a more even slope and direct water flow
- Contouring involves creating specific shapes and contours on the land surface to control water movement and promote infiltration

  b. Importance of Proper Grading
- Proper grading ensures that water flows away from structures, such as your home's foundation, and into designated drainage areas
- Improper grading can lead to water accumulation, foundation damage, and other drainage issues

  c. Grading Techniques
- Cut and Fill: This technique involves removing soil from high points (cut) and adding it to low points (fill) to create a more even slope

- Slope Modification: Adjusting the slope of your yard to achieve the recommended 1-2% grade for proper drainage
- Terracing: Creating a series of level steps or platforms on steep slopes to slow down water flow and prevent soil erosion

d. Contouring Techniques

- Swales: Shallow, linear depressions that are designed to channel water flow and promote infiltration
- Berms: Raised mounds of soil that can be used to direct water flow and create barriers to prevent water from reaching certain areas
- Retention Basins: Shallow depressions in the landscape that are designed to temporarily hold and infiltrate water during heavy rainfall events

e. Grading and Contouring Best Practices

- Ensure a minimum slope of 1-2% away from structures for proper drainage
- Maintain a slope of 6 inches for every 10 feet (5% slope) around your home's foundation
- Avoid creating steep slopes (>5%) that can contribute to soil erosion and reduced infiltration
- Use erosion control measures, such as mulch, vegetation, or erosion control blankets, on newly graded areas until they are stabilized
- Consider the natural drainage patterns of your yard and work with them when possible
- Ensure that grading and contouring direct water flow into appropriate drainage outlets, such as swales, catch basins, or storm sewer systems

Site Preparation for Grading and Contouring
a. Soil Testing
- Conduct a soil test to determine the type and characteristics of your yard's soil
- Soil type and compaction can affect the success of grading and contouring efforts

b. Utility Location
- Contact local utility companies to mark the location of underground utilities, such as gas lines, water mains, and electrical cables
- Avoid grading or excavating in areas with underground utilities to prevent damage and ensure safety

c. Vegetation Removal
- Remove any vegetation, such as grass, shrubs, or trees, that may interfere with grading and contouring
- Properly dispose of removed vegetation or use it for composting or mulching

d. Erosion Control Measures
- Install temporary erosion control measures, such as silt fences or straw bales, to prevent soil erosion during the grading process
- These measures help to keep sediment and debris from entering nearby water bodies or storm sewer systems

Implementing Grading and Contouring
a. Equipment and Tools
- Grading and contouring typically require the use of heavy equipment, such as excavators, skid steers, and bulldozers
- Smaller projects may be accomplished with hand tools, such as shovels, rakes, and wheelbarrows

b. Grading Process
- Begin by marking the areas where cut and fill will be necessary to achieve the desired slope and contours
- Use stakes and string lines to establish the new grade and ensure a consistent slope
- Remove soil from high points and add it to low points, compacting the soil as needed to ensure stability

c. Contouring Process
- Use stakes and string lines to mark the desired contours, such as swales, berms, or retention basins
- Excavate or build up the soil to create the desired shapes and contours
- Ensure that the contours are smooth and consistent, with no abrupt changes in elevation

d. Finishing and Stabilization
- Once grading and contouring are complete, smooth the soil surface with a rake or grading blade
- Apply mulch, seed, or sod to the newly graded areas to prevent soil erosion and promote vegetation growth
- Water the area thoroughly and monitor it regularly until the vegetation is well-established

Maintenance and Monitoring

a. Regular Inspections
- Periodically inspect the graded and contoured areas to ensure that they are functioning properly and directing water flow as intended
- Look for signs of soil erosion, water accumulation, or damage to the contours

b. Erosion Control
- Maintain erosion control measures, such as mulch or vegetation, to prevent soil erosion and ensure the stability of the graded areas
- Replace or repair any damaged erosion control measures promptly

c. Vegetation Management
- Regularly mow, trim, and maintain the vegetation in the graded and contoured areas to promote healthy growth and prevent overcrowding
- Remove any invasive or unwanted plant species that may interfere with drainage or compete with desired vegetation

d. Sediment Removal
- Over time, sediment and debris may accumulate in swales, retention basins, or other drainage features
- Regularly remove accumulated sediment to maintain the effectiveness of the drainage system and prevent blockages

By understanding and implementing proper grading and contouring techniques, you can effectively manage surface water runoff and prevent drainage issues in your yard. These techniques, combined with other surface drainage solutions like swales, berms, and retention basins, form a comprehensive approach to managing water flow and promoting healthy, well-drained landscapes.

Swales and Berms

Swales and berms are two essential surface drainage techniques that can be used in conjunction with grading and contouring to manage water runoff and prevent drainage issues in your yard. Swales are shallow, linear depressions that are designed to channel water flow and promote infiltration, while berms are raised mounds of soil that can be used to direct water flow and create barriers to prevent water from reaching certain areas. In this section, we'll explore swales and berms in detail, including their design, construction, and maintenance.

a. Swales
  i. Definition and Function
- Swales are shallow, linear depressions in the landscape that are designed to collect, channel, and infiltrate water runoff
- They are typically vegetated with grass or other plants to slow down water flow, promote infiltration, and filter pollutants
- Swales can be used to direct water flow away from structures and into appropriate drainage areas, such as retention basins or storm sewer systems
  ii. Types of Swales
- Grassed Swales: These are shallow, vegetated channels that are designed to convey and infiltrate water runoff
- Bioswales: These are similar to grassed swales but are planted with a variety of native plants and grasses to enhance water filtration and improve biodiversity

- Infiltration Swales: These are designed to collect and infiltrate water runoff into the underlying soil, rather than conveying it to a drainage outlet

iii. Designing Swales
- Swales should be sized and shaped based on the expected water runoff volume and the soil infiltration rate
- A typical swale has a trapezoidal or parabolic cross-section, with a flat bottom and gently sloping sides (3:1 to 5:1 slope)
- The length and width of the swale should be based on the drainage area and the desired water velocity
- Swales should have a minimum slope of 1% to ensure proper drainage and prevent water stagnation

iv. Constructing Swales
- Begin by marking the location and shape of the swale using stakes and string lines
- Excavate the swale to the desired depth and shape, ensuring that the bottom is level and the sides have the appropriate slope
- If necessary, install erosion control measures, such as erosion control blankets or turf reinforcement mats, to prevent soil erosion
- Plant the swale with appropriate vegetation, such as grass or native plants, to promote infiltration and filtration

v. Maintaining Swales
- Regularly inspect the swale for signs of erosion, sediment accumulation, or damage to the vegetation
- Remove any accumulated sediment or debris to maintain the swale's water conveyance capacity

- Mow or trim the vegetation as needed to maintain the desired height and prevent overcrowding
- Repair any eroded or damaged areas promptly to prevent further deterioration

b. Berms
i. Definition and Function
- Berms are raised mounds of soil that are used to direct water flow, create barriers, or provide visual interest in the landscape
- They can be used to prevent water from reaching certain areas, such as structures or low-lying areas prone to water accumulation
- Berms can also be used to create a natural-looking boundary or to provide privacy and noise reduction

ii. Types of Berms
- Diversion Berms: These are designed to intercept and divert water runoff away from structures or sensitive areas
- Containment Berms: These are used to create a barrier around areas that may be prone to flooding or water accumulation, such as low-lying areas or retention basins
- Aesthetic Berms: These are used primarily for visual interest and can be planted with a variety of trees, shrubs, and groundcovers

iii. Designing Berms
- Berms should be designed based on the intended function, the available space, and the surrounding landscape features
- The height and width of the berm should be proportional to the size of the area and the desired level of protection or visual impact

- Berms should have gentle slopes (3:1 to 5:1) to ensure stability and prevent soil erosion
- The top of the berm should be slightly crowned to promote water runoff and prevent water from ponding on the surface

iv. Constructing Berms

- Begin by marking the location and shape of the berm using stakes and string lines
- Use clean, compacted fill soil to build up the berm to the desired height and shape
- Ensure that the soil is well-compacted to prevent settling and maintain the berm's shape over time
- Cover the berm with topsoil and plant with appropriate vegetation, such as grass, groundcovers, or shrubs

v. Maintaining Berms

- Regularly inspect the berm for signs of erosion, settling, or damage to the vegetation
- Repair any eroded or damaged areas promptly to prevent further deterioration
- Mow or trim the vegetation as needed to maintain the desired height and shape
- Monitor the berm's performance during heavy rainfall events to ensure that it is effectively directing water flow and preventing water accumulation

By incorporating swales and berms into your yard's drainage plan, you can effectively manage water runoff, prevent drainage issues, and create a more visually appealing landscape. These techniques can be used in combination with other surface drainage solutions, such as grading and contouring, to create a comprehensive and effective drainage system.

Proper design, construction, and maintenance of swales and berms are essential to ensure their long-term performance and effectiveness in managing water runoff and preventing drainage issues.

French Drains and Trench Drains

French drains and trench drains are two types of subsurface drainage systems that are used to collect and redirect water runoff away from structures and low-lying areas in your yard. These systems are designed to intercept water below the surface and channel it to a suitable drainage outlet, such as a storm sewer or retention basin. In this section, we'll explore French drains and trench drains in detail, including their design, construction, and maintenance.

a. French Drains
  i. Definition and Function
- French drains are subsurface drainage systems that consist of a perforated pipe surrounded by gravel or crushed stone
- They are designed to collect and redirect groundwater or surface water runoff away from structures and low-lying areas
- French drains can be used to address a variety of drainage issues, such as water accumulation near foundations, wet basements, or saturated soil in landscaped areas

  ii. Components of a French Drain
- Perforated Pipe: This is the main component of a French drain and is typically made of flexible, corrugated plastic with small holes or slots to allow water to enter
- Gravel or Crushed Stone: The perforated pipe is surrounded by a layer of gravel or crushed stone, which acts as a filter to prevent soil and debris from clogging the pipe

- Geotextile Fabric: A layer of geotextile fabric is often placed around the gravel or crushed stone to prevent fine soil particles from entering the drain and clogging the pipe
- Drainage Outlet: The French drain must have a suitable outlet, such as a storm sewer, retention basin, or daylight point, to discharge the collected water

iii. Designing French Drains
- French drains should be designed based on the specific drainage needs of your yard, including the size of the drainage area, the soil type, and the expected water volume
- The perforated pipe should be sized based on the expected water flow rate and should have a minimum slope of 1% to ensure proper drainage
- The trench for the French drain should be deep enough to intercept the water table or the desired drainage depth, typically 18 to 24 inches
- The trench should be wide enough to accommodate the perforated pipe and a sufficient layer of gravel or crushed stone, typically 6 to 12 inches

iv. Constructing French Drains
- Begin by marking the location and path of the French drain using stakes and string lines
- Excavate the trench to the desired depth and width, ensuring that the bottom of the trench has a consistent slope towards the drainage outlet
- Line the trench with geotextile fabric to prevent soil intrusion and wrap the fabric around the perforated pipe to prevent clogging

- Place the perforated pipe in the trench, ensuring that it has a consistent slope and is oriented with the perforations facing downward
- Surround the pipe with a layer of gravel or crushed stone, filling the trench to within a few inches of the surface
- Cover the gravel or crushed stone with a layer of geotextile fabric and backfill the remaining space with soil

v. Maintaining French Drains
- Regularly inspect the French drain outlet to ensure that it is free of obstructions and is discharging water properly
- Remove any accumulated sediment or debris from the outlet to prevent blockages and maintain the drain's effectiveness
- Monitor the French drain's performance during heavy rainfall events to ensure that it is effectively collecting and redirecting water
- If the French drain becomes clogged or damaged, it may need to be excavated and repaired or replaced

b. Trench Drains

i. Definition and Function
- Trench drains are shallow, linear drainage systems that are used to collect and redirect surface water runoff
- They are typically installed in paved areas, such as driveways, patios, or walkways, to prevent water from ponding or flowing towards structures
- Trench drains can also be used in landscaped areas to collect and redirect water runoff from high-traffic or erosion-prone areas

ii. Components of a Trench Drain
- Channel: The main component of a trench drain is a preformed or cast-in-place concrete channel that is designed to collect and convey water
- Grate: The channel is covered with a removable grate, which allows water to enter the drain while preventing debris and safety hazards
- Drainage Outlet: The trench drain must have a suitable outlet, such as a catch basin or a connection to a storm sewer, to discharge the collected water

iii. Designing Trench Drains
- Trench drains should be designed based on the specific drainage needs of the area, including the size of the drainage area, the expected water volume, and the desired aesthetic appearance
- The channel should be sized based on the expected water flow rate and should have a minimum slope of 1% to ensure proper drainage
- The grate should be selected based on the expected traffic load and the desired visual appearance, with options ranging from simple steel grates to decorative cast iron or bronze grates
- The trench drain should be located and oriented to effectively intercept and redirect surface water runoff away from structures and low-lying areas

iv. Constructing Trench Drains
- Begin by marking the location and path of the trench drain using stakes and string lines
- Excavate the trench to the desired depth and width, ensuring that the bottom of the trench has a consistent slope towards the drainage outlet

- Install the pre-formed channel or construct the cast-in-place channel, ensuring that it has a consistent slope and is properly aligned
- Connect the channel to the drainage outlet, using a catch basin or a direct connection to the storm sewer
- Install the grate over the channel, ensuring that it is properly seated and secured
- Backfill around the channel and grate with concrete or paving material, as appropriate

v. Maintaining Trench Drains

- Regularly inspect the trench drain and grate to ensure that they are free of obstructions and are functioning properly
- Remove any accumulated sediment, debris, or vegetation from the channel and grate to prevent blockages and maintain the drain's effectiveness
- Monitor the trench drain's performance during heavy rainfall events to ensure that it is effectively collecting and redirecting surface water runoff
- If the trench drain becomes damaged or deteriorated, it may need to be repaired or replaced to maintain its effectiveness

By incorporating French drains and trench drains into your yard's drainage plan, you can effectively collect and redirect subsurface and surface water runoff away from structures and low-lying areas. These systems can be used in combination with other drainage solutions, such as grading, swales, and berms, to create a comprehensive and effective drainage plan. Proper design, construction, and maintenance of French drains and trench drains are essential to ensure their long-term performance and effectiveness in managing water runoff and preventing drainage issues in your yard.

Catch Basins and Grates

Catch basins and grates are essential components of a yard drainage system that are used to collect and convey surface water runoff into underground drainage pipes or storm sewers. They are typically installed in low-lying areas, such as at the bottom of slopes or in paved areas, to prevent water from ponding or flowing towards structures. In this section, we'll explore catch basins and grates in detail, including their design, construction, and maintenance.

a. Catch Basins
 i. Definition and Function
- Catch basins are subsurface drainage structures that are designed to collect and convey surface water runoff into underground drainage pipes or storm sewers
- They are typically installed in low-lying areas or at the bottom of slopes to intercept and redirect surface water runoff away from structures and landscaped areas
- Catch basins also serve as a sediment and debris trap, helping to prevent blockages and maintain the effectiveness of the drainage system

 ii. Components of a Catch Basin
- Basin: The main component of a catch basin is a pre-cast or cast-in-place concrete basin that is designed to collect and temporarily store surface water runoff
- Inlet: The basin has one or more inlets, which are openings that allow surface water runoff to enter the basin
- Outlet: The basin also has an outlet, which is a pipe or opening that allows the collected water to flow into the underground drainage system or storm sewer

- Sump: Some catch basins include a sump, which is a deeper section of the basin that is designed to trap sediment and debris

iii. Designing Catch Basins
- Catch basins should be designed based on the specific drainage needs of the area, including the size of the drainage area, the expected water volume, and the capacity of the downstream drainage system
- The basin should be sized to accommodate the expected water flow rate and to provide sufficient storage capacity to prevent overflows during heavy rainfall events
- The inlet and outlet should be sized and located to effectively intercept and convey surface water runoff into the basin and the downstream drainage system
- The sump, if included, should be designed to provide sufficient storage capacity for trapped sediment and debris

iv. Constructing Catch Basins
- Begin by excavating the area where the catch basin will be installed, ensuring that the excavation is deep enough to accommodate the basin and any connecting pipes
- Place a layer of compacted gravel or crushed stone at the bottom of the excavation to provide a stable base for the basin
- Install the pre-cast or construct the cast-in-place basin, ensuring that it is level and properly aligned with the incoming and outgoing drainage pipes
- Connect the basin to the drainage pipes, using flexible or rigid couplings as appropriate
- Install the grate or cover over the basin, ensuring that it is properly seated and secured

- Backfill around the basin with compacted soil or gravel, as appropriate

v. Maintaining Catch Basins
- Regularly inspect the catch basin and grate to ensure that they are free of obstructions and are functioning properly
- Remove any accumulated sediment, debris, or vegetation from the basin and sump to prevent blockages and maintain the basin's effectiveness
- Monitor the catch basin's performance during heavy rainfall events to ensure that it is effectively collecting and conveying surface water runoff
- If the catch basin becomes damaged or deteriorated, it may need to be repaired or replaced to maintain its effectiveness

b. Grates

i. Definition and Function
- Grates are removable covers that are installed over catch basins, trench drains, and other drainage structures to allow surface water runoff to enter the drainage system while preventing debris and safety hazards
- They are typically made of metal, such as steel or cast iron, and are designed to withstand the expected traffic loads and environmental conditions
- Grates also serve an aesthetic function, with options ranging from simple, utilitarian designs to decorative, ornamental patterns

ii. Types of Grates
- Bar Grates: These are the most common type of grate and consist of a series of parallel bars or rods that are spaced to allow water to pass through while preventing larger debris from entering the drainage system
- Perforated Grates: These grates have a series of small holes or perforations that allow water to pass through while preventing smaller debris from entering the drainage system
- Decorative Grates: These grates feature ornamental patterns or designs that are used to enhance the visual appearance of the drainage system while still providing effective water collection and conveyance

iii. Selecting Grates
- Grates should be selected based on the specific needs of the area, including the expected traffic loads, the desired visual appearance, and the size of the drainage opening
- The grate should be sized to effectively cover the drainage opening while allowing sufficient water flow into the drainage system
- The grate material should be selected based on the expected traffic loads and environmental conditions, with options ranging from lightweight plastic grates for pedestrian areas to heavy-duty steel or cast iron grates for vehicular traffic
- The grate pattern should be selected to provide the desired balance of water collection, debris prevention, and visual appearance

iv. Installing Grates
- Grates are typically installed over catch basins, trench drains, or other drainage structures during the construction process
- The grate should be properly seated and secured to the drainage structure, using bolts, screws, or other fasteners as appropriate
- The grate should be installed level with the surrounding surface to prevent tripping hazards and to ensure proper water flow into the drainage system

v. Maintaining Grates
- Regularly inspect the grate to ensure that it is properly seated and secured and that it is free of damage or corrosion
- Remove any accumulated debris or vegetation from the grate to prevent blockages and maintain the grate's effectiveness
- Replace any damaged or missing grates promptly to maintain the safety and effectiveness of the drainage system

By incorporating catch basins and grates into your yard's drainage plan, you can effectively collect and convey surface water runoff into underground drainage systems while preventing debris and safety hazards. These components can be used in combination with other drainage solutions, such as French drains, trench drains, and swales, to create a comprehensive and effective drainage plan. Proper design, construction, and maintenance of catch basins and grates are essential to ensure their long-term performance and effectiveness in managing water runoff and preventing drainage issues in your yard.

Subsurface Drainage Methods
Perforated Pipes and Drainage Tiles

Subsurface drainage methods are designed to remove excess water from the soil profile, preventing waterlogging and promoting healthy plant growth. These methods involve installing perforated pipes or drainage tiles below the surface to intercept and convey excess water away from the affected area. In this section, we'll explore perforated pipes and drainage tiles in detail, including their design, installation, and maintenance.

Perforated Pipes and Drainage Tiles
 a. Definition and Function
- Perforated pipes and drainage tiles are subsurface drainage components that are used to collect and convey excess water away from poorly drained soils
- They are typically installed in a network of trenches or beds that are excavated to a depth that intercepts the water table or the zone of soil saturation
- The perforations or openings in the pipes or tiles allow water to enter the drainage system while preventing soil particles from clogging the pipes

 b. Types of Perforated Pipes and Drainage Tiles
- Corrugated Plastic Pipes: These are the most common type of perforated pipe and are made from lightweight, flexible plastic materials such as polyethylene (PE) or polyvinyl chloride (PVC)
- Clay Tiles: These are traditional drainage tiles that are made from fired clay and have a cylindrical or horseshoe-shaped cross-section with perforations or gaps between the tiles

- Concrete Tiles: These are similar to clay tiles but are made from precast concrete and have a wider range of sizes and shapes available
- Perforated PVC Pipes: These are rigid, smooth-walled pipes that are made from PVC and have precisely spaced perforations for efficient water collection and conveyance

c. Designing Perforated Pipe and Drainage Tile Systems
- The design of a perforated pipe or drainage tile system depends on several factors, including the soil type, water table depth, slope, and drainage area size
- The pipe or tile size and spacing should be selected based on the expected water flow rate and the soil hydraulic conductivity, with larger pipes or closer spacing used for higher flow rates or less permeable soils
- The depth and slope of the drainage trenches or beds should be designed to effectively intercept and convey excess water while minimizing the disturbance to the surrounding soil and vegetation
- The outlet of the drainage system should be designed to safely convey the collected water to a suitable discharge point, such as a storm sewer, detention basin, or vegetated swale

d. Installing Perforated Pipes and Drainage Tiles
- Begin by excavating the drainage trenches or beds to the designed depth and slope, ensuring that the bottom of the trench is smooth and free of rocks or debris
- Place a layer of permeable geotextile fabric or gravel bedding in the bottom of the trench to prevent soil intrusion and provide a stable base for the pipes or tiles

- Install the perforated pipes or drainage tiles in the trench, ensuring that they are properly aligned and connected using appropriate couplings or fittings
- Cover the pipes or tiles with a layer of permeable geotextile fabric or gravel to prevent soil intrusion and promote water flow into the drainage system
- Backfill the trench with permeable soil or gravel, taking care not to damage or dislodge the pipes or tiles during the backfilling process
- Install any necessary outlet structures, such as cleanouts, observation wells, or outlet pipes, to facilitate maintenance and monitoring of the drainage system

e. Maintaining Perforated Pipes and Drainage Tiles
- Regularly inspect the outlet of the drainage system to ensure that it is free of obstructions and is discharging water properly
- Remove any accumulated sediment or debris from the outlet or cleanouts to prevent blockages and maintain the system's effectiveness
- Monitor the performance of the drainage system during wet periods to ensure that it is effectively removing excess water from the soil profile
- If the drainage system becomes clogged or damaged, it may need to be excavated and repaired or replaced to restore its functionality

By incorporating perforated pipes and drainage tiles into your yard's subsurface drainage plan, you can effectively remove excess water from poorly drained soils, preventing waterlogging and promoting healthy plant growth.

These components can be used in combination with other drainage solutions, such as French drains, dry wells, or sump pumps, to create a comprehensive and effective subsurface drainage system. Proper design, installation, and maintenance of perforated pipes and drainage tiles are essential to ensure their long-term performance and effectiveness in managing subsurface water and preventing drainage issues in your yard.

Dry Wells and Soakaways

Dry wells and soakaways are subsurface drainage structures that are designed to collect and infiltrate stormwater runoff, reducing the volume and rate of runoff that enters the downstream drainage system. They are typically used in areas with well-draining soils and can be an effective way to manage stormwater on-site, recharge groundwater, and reduce the burden on municipal drainage infrastructure. In this section, we'll explore dry wells and soakaways in detail, including their design, installation, and maintenance.

a. Dry Wells

i. Definition and Function
- A dry well is a subsurface drainage structure that is designed to collect and infiltrate stormwater runoff from roofs, driveways, or other impervious surfaces
- It typically consists of a large, excavated pit that is filled with gravel or other porous material and is lined with a permeable geotextile fabric
- The stormwater runoff enters the dry well through an inlet pipe or surface grate and gradually infiltrates into the surrounding soil, reducing the volume and rate of runoff that enters the downstream drainage system

ii. Design Considerations
- The size and depth of the dry well should be based on the expected volume and rate of stormwater runoff, as well as the infiltration capacity of the surrounding soil
- The dry well should be located at least 10 feet away from building foundations and property lines to prevent water damage and conflicts with adjacent structures

- The inlet pipe or surface grate should be sized to accommodate the expected flow rate and should be equipped with a debris screen or sediment trap to prevent clogging
- The dry well should be designed with an overflow pipe or spillway to safely convey excess runoff to the downstream drainage system during extreme rainfall events

iii. Installation Process
- Begin by excavating the dry well pit to the designed depth and dimensions, ensuring that the bottom of the pit is level and free of rocks or debris
- Line the pit with a permeable geotextile fabric to prevent soil intrusion and maintain the porosity of the gravel fill
- Install the inlet pipe or surface grate, ensuring that it is properly connected to the dry well and is equipped with a debris screen or sediment trap
- Fill the pit with clean, washed gravel or other porous material, taking care to avoid compacting the fill material or damaging the geotextile fabric
- Install the overflow pipe or spillway, ensuring that it is properly connected to the downstream drainage system and is sized to accommodate the expected flow rate
- Cover the top of the dry well with a layer of geotextile fabric and backfill with topsoil or other suitable material, leaving the inlet pipe or surface grate exposed for maintenance access

iv. Maintenance Requirements
- Regularly inspect the inlet pipe or surface grate to ensure that it is free of debris and sediment and is allowing stormwater to enter the dry well freely

- Remove any accumulated sediment or debris from the inlet pipe or surface grate to prevent clogging and maintain the system's effectiveness
- Monitor the performance of the dry well during rainfall events to ensure that it is effectively infiltrating stormwater and reducing runoff volume and rate
- If the dry well becomes clogged or fails to infiltrate stormwater properly, it may need to be excavated and cleaned or replaced to restore its functionality

b. Soakaways

i. Definition and Function

- A soakaway is a subsurface drainage structure that is similar to a dry well but is typically smaller in size and is designed to infiltrate stormwater runoff from a single source, such as a roof downspout or small paved area
- It typically consists of a small, excavated pit that is filled with gravel or other porous material and is lined with a permeable geotextile fabric
- The stormwater runoff enters the soakaway through an inlet pipe and gradually infiltrates into the surrounding soil, reducing the volume and rate of runoff that enters the downstream drainage system

ii. Design Considerations

- The size and depth of the soakaway should be based on the expected volume and rate of stormwater runoff, as well as the infiltration capacity of the surrounding soil
- The soakaway should be located at least 5 feet away from building foundations and property lines to prevent water damage and conflicts with adjacent structures

- The inlet pipe should be sized to accommodate the expected flow rate and should be equipped with a debris screen or sediment trap to prevent clogging
- The soakaway should be designed with an overflow pipe or surface outlet to safely convey excess runoff to the downstream drainage system during extreme rainfall events

iii. Installation Process
- Begin by excavating the soakaway pit to the designed depth and dimensions, ensuring that the bottom of the pit is level and free of rocks or debris
- Line the pit with a permeable geotextile fabric to prevent soil intrusion and maintain the porosity of the gravel fill
- Install the inlet pipe, ensuring that it is properly connected to the soakaway and is equipped with a debris screen or sediment trap
- Fill the pit with clean, washed gravel or other porous material, taking care to avoid compacting the fill material or damaging the geotextile fabric
- Install the overflow pipe or surface outlet, ensuring that it is properly connected to the downstream drainage system and is sized to accommodate the expected flow rate
- Cover the top of the soakaway with a layer of geotextile fabric and backfill with topsoil or other suitable material, leaving the inlet pipe exposed for maintenance access

iv. Maintenance Requirements
- Regularly inspect the inlet pipe to ensure that it is free of debris and sediment and is allowing stormwater to enter the soakaway freely

- Remove any accumulated sediment or debris from the inlet pipe to prevent clogging and maintain the system's effectiveness
- Monitor the performance of the soakaway during rainfall events to ensure that it is effectively infiltrating stormwater and reducing runoff volume and rate
- If the soakaway becomes clogged or fails to infiltrate stormwater properly, it may need to be excavated and cleaned or replaced to restore its functionality

By incorporating dry wells and soakaways into your yard's stormwater management plan, you can effectively reduce the volume and rate of runoff that enters the downstream drainage system, recharge groundwater, and minimize the impacts of development on the natural hydrologic cycle. These structures can be used in combination with other stormwater management practices, such as rain gardens, permeable pavement, and green roofs, to create a comprehensive and sustainable approach to stormwater management. Proper design, installation, and maintenance of dry wells and soakaways are essential to ensure their long-term performance and effectiveness in managing stormwater runoff and preventing drainage issues in your yard.

Sump Pumps and Lift Stations

Sump pumps and lift stations are mechanical devices that are used to remove water from low-lying areas or underground spaces where gravity drainage is not feasible. They are typically used in basements, crawl spaces, or other areas that are prone to flooding or water accumulation, and can be an effective way to prevent water damage and maintain a dry and usable space. In this section, we'll explore sump pumps and lift stations in detail, including their design, installation, and maintenance.

a. Sump Pumps
  i. Definition and Function
- A sump pump is a mechanical device that is designed to remove water from a sump pit, which is a small, excavated area in the lowest part of a basement or crawl space
- The sump pit collects water from the surrounding soil or from foundation drains and the sump pump automatically pumps the water out of the pit and away from the building when the water level rises above a certain point
- Sump pumps are typically powered by electricity and can be either submersible (installed inside the sump pit) or pedestal (installed above the sump pit)

  ii. Types of Sump Pumps
- Submersible Sump Pumps: These pumps are designed to be installed inside the sump pit and are fully submerged in water when operating. They are quieter and more efficient than pedestal pumps but can be more difficult to access for maintenance.

- Pedestal Sump Pumps: These pumps are designed to be installed above the sump pit and have a motor that is mounted on a pedestal above the water level. They are less expensive and easier to maintain than submersible pumps but are louder and less efficient.
- Battery Backup Sump Pumps: These pumps are designed to operate on battery power in the event of a power outage, providing an added level of protection against flooding and water damage.

iii. Installation Considerations
- The size and capacity of the sump pump should be based on the expected volume and rate of water inflow, as well as the depth and size of the sump pit
- The sump pump should be installed in a sump pit that is at least 24 inches deep and 18 inches wide, with a solid bottom and a cover to prevent debris and pests from entering the pit
- The discharge pipe should be properly sized and routed to a suitable outlet point, such as a storm sewer or drainage swale, and should be equipped with a check valve to prevent backflow
- The sump pump should be connected to a dedicated electrical circuit with a ground fault circuit interrupter (GFCI) to prevent electrical hazards and ensure reliable operation

iv. Maintenance Requirements
- Regularly inspect the sump pump and sump pit to ensure that they are free of debris and sediment and are operating properly
- Test the sump pump periodically by manually filling the sump pit with water and verifying that the pump activates and removes the water effectively

- Clean the sump pump and sump pit annually or as needed to remove any accumulated debris or sediment that could clog the pump or impede its operation
- Replace the sump pump every 5-7 years or as recommended by the manufacturer to ensure reliable and efficient operation

b. Lift Stations
i. Definition and Function
- A lift station is a mechanical device that is designed to pump wastewater or stormwater from a low-lying area to a higher elevation where it can be discharged by gravity
- Lift stations are typically used in areas where the topography or elevation of the land prevents gravity drainage, such as in flat or low-lying areas or where the discharge point is located at a higher elevation than the collection point
- Lift stations can be used for a variety of applications, including municipal wastewater collection, stormwater management, and agricultural irrigation

ii. Types of Lift Stations
- Wet Well Lift Stations: These lift stations consist of a wet well (a large, underground tank) that collects the wastewater or stormwater and one or more submersible pumps that are installed inside the wet well to pump the water to a higher elevation

- Dry Well Lift Stations: These lift stations consist of a dry well (a large, underground vault) that houses the pumps and other mechanical equipment, and a separate wet well that collects the wastewater or stormwater and feeds it to the dry well through a series of pipes and valves
- Packaged Lift Stations: These lift stations are pre-manufactured units that include the wet well, pumps, and other mechanical equipment in a single, self-contained package that can be easily installed and commissioned

iii. Installation Considerations
- The size and capacity of the lift station should be based on the expected volume and rate of wastewater or stormwater inflow, as well as the elevation difference between the collection point and the discharge point
- The lift station should be installed in a location that is easily accessible for maintenance and repair, and should be equipped with suitable access hatches, ladders, and other safety features
- The discharge pipe should be properly sized and routed to the discharge point, and should be equipped with suitable valves, fittings, and other appurtenances to control the flow and prevent backflow
- The lift station should be connected to a suitable power supply and control system, and should be equipped with backup power and alarm systems to ensure reliable and safe operation

iv. Maintenance Requirements
- Regularly inspect the lift station and its components to ensure that they are free of debris and sediment and are operating properly
- Test the pumps and other mechanical equipment periodically to verify that they are functioning properly and are delivering the required flow and pressure
- Clean the wet well and other components annually or as needed to remove any accumulated debris or sediment that could clog the pumps or impede their operation
- Replace the pumps and other mechanical equipment as recommended by the manufacturer to ensure reliable and efficient operation over the long term

By incorporating sump pumps and lift stations into your yard's drainage and stormwater management plan, you can effectively remove water from low-lying areas or underground spaces where gravity drainage is not feasible, prevent water damage, and maintain a dry and usable space. These mechanical devices can be used in combination with other drainage solutions, such as French drains, dry wells, and soakaways, to create a comprehensive and effective approach to water management. Proper design, installation, and maintenance of sump pumps and lift stations are essential to ensure their long-term performance and effectiveness in managing water and preventing drainage issues in your yard.

Choosing the Right Drainage Solution for Your Yard

Selecting the appropriate drainage solution for your yard is crucial to effectively manage water runoff, prevent water damage, and maintain a healthy and attractive landscape. The right drainage solution will depend on a variety of factors, including the specific drainage issues you are facing, the size and layout of your yard, the soil type and topography, and your budget and maintenance preferences. In this section, we'll explore the key considerations for choosing the right drainage solution for your yard and provide guidance on how to evaluate and select the best option for your needs.

a. Assessing Your Yard's Drainage Issues
  i. Identifying Problem Areas
- The first step in choosing the right drainage solution is to identify the specific areas of your yard that are experiencing drainage problems, such as standing water, soggy soil, or erosion
- Look for signs of poor drainage, such as water stains on walls or foundations, wet or spongy soil, or dead or struggling plants
- Note the location, size, and severity of each problem area, as well as any nearby structures, utilities, or other features that may be affected by the drainage issues

  ii. Determining the Cause of Drainage Problems
- Once you have identified the problem areas, the next step is to determine the underlying cause of the drainage issues, such as poor grading, soil compaction, or insufficient drainage infrastructure

- Consider factors such as the slope and contours of your yard, the type and condition of your soil, and the presence of any existing drainage systems or features
- Consult with a professional landscaper, drainage contractor, or civil engineer if needed to accurately diagnose the cause of your drainage problems and recommend appropriate solutions

b. Evaluating Drainage Solution Options
i. Surface Drainage Solutions
- Surface drainage solutions, such as grading, swales, and berms, are designed to direct water away from problem areas and into appropriate drainage channels or retention areas
- These solutions are typically less expensive and easier to install than subsurface solutions, but may require more ongoing maintenance and may not be suitable for all soil types or yard layouts
- Consider factors such as the size and slope of your yard, the amount of water runoff, and the desired appearance and functionality of your landscape when evaluating surface drainage options

ii. Subsurface Drainage Solutions
- Subsurface drainage solutions, such as French drains, curtain drains, and sump pumps, are designed to collect and remove water from below the surface of your yard before it can cause damage or problems
- These solutions are typically more effective and reliable than surface solutions, but may be more expensive and complex to install and maintain

- Consider factors such as the depth and extent of your drainage problems, the soil type and water table, and the proximity of structures and utilities when evaluating subsurface drainage options

iii. Stormwater Management Solutions
- Stormwater management solutions, such as rain gardens, bioswales, and permeable pavement, are designed to capture, filter, and infiltrate water runoff on-site, reducing the volume and velocity of water that enters the drainage system
- These solutions can provide multiple benefits, such as improving water quality, recharging groundwater, and enhancing the aesthetic and ecological value of your landscape
- Consider factors such as the size and layout of your yard, the amount and quality of water runoff, and your goals for sustainability and environmental stewardship when evaluating stormwater management options

c. Selecting the Best Drainage Solution
i. Prioritizing Your Needs and Goals
- Before selecting a drainage solution, it's important to prioritize your needs and goals for your yard, such as improving functionality, enhancing aesthetics, or reducing maintenance requirements
- Consider factors such as your budget, timeline, and level of expertise, as well as any local regulations or permit requirements that may affect your options
- Rank your priorities and use them to guide your evaluation and selection process, focusing on solutions that best meet your most important needs and goals

ii. Evaluating the Pros and Cons of Each Option
- For each drainage solution option that you are considering, evaluate the pros and cons based on factors such as effectiveness, cost, durability, maintenance requirements, and environmental impact
- Consider the specific characteristics and constraints of your yard, such as soil type, slope, and climate, and how they may affect the performance and suitability of each option
- Consult with professionals, such as landscapers, drainage contractors, or civil engineers, to get expert advice and recommendations based on your specific needs and circumstances

iii. Making a Decision and Implementing the Solution
- Based on your evaluation of the pros and cons and your prioritized needs and goals, select the drainage solution that offers the best overall value and performance for your yard
- Develop a plan for implementing the solution, including any necessary permits, materials, equipment, and labor, and establish a timeline and budget for the project
- Consider hiring professionals to assist with the design, installation, and maintenance of the drainage solution, particularly for complex or large-scale projects
- Monitor the performance of the drainage solution over time and make any necessary adjustments or repairs to ensure its continued effectiveness and longevity

By carefully assessing your yard's drainage issues, evaluating the available drainage solution options, and selecting the best option based on your specific needs and goals, you can effectively address drainage problems and maintain a healthy, functional, and attractive landscape. Whether you choose a surface drainage solution, a subsurface drainage solution, or a stormwater management solution, the key is to choose a solution that is well-suited to your yard's unique characteristics and constraints and that provides reliable, long-term performance with minimal maintenance requirements.

Chapter 3
Landscaping Techniques for Improved Drainage

Rain Gardens and Bioswales

Rain gardens and bioswales are landscaping techniques that are designed to capture, filter, and infiltrate stormwater runoff on-site, reducing the volume and velocity of water that enters the drainage system and improving the quality of water that eventually reaches local waterways. These techniques use a combination of plants, soil, and gravel to create a natural filtration system that mimics the hydrologic functions of undeveloped landscapes. In this section, we'll explore rain gardens and bioswales in detail, including their design, installation, and maintenance.

a. Rain Gardens

i. Definition and Function

- A rain garden is a shallow, landscaped depression that is designed to capture and infiltrate stormwater runoff from roofs, driveways, and other impervious surfaces
- Rain gardens are typically planted with a variety of native plants, grasses, and shrubs that are adapted to the local climate and soil conditions and that can tolerate both wet and dry conditions
- The plants in a rain garden help to filter pollutants, such as sediment, nutrients, and heavy metals, from the stormwater runoff, while the soil and gravel layers help to slow down the water and promote infiltration into the ground

ii. Design Considerations
- The size and shape of a rain garden should be based on the size of the contributing drainage area, the amount of impervious surface, and the soil type and infiltration rate
- A typical rain garden is sized to capture and infiltrate the first inch of rainfall from the contributing drainage area, which accounts for the majority of rainfall events in most regions
- The depth of a rain garden should be between 6 and 12 inches, with a flat bottom and gently sloping sides to allow for even distribution and infiltration of water
- The soil in a rain garden should be a well-draining, sandy loam mix that is amended with compost or other organic matter to improve its structure and fertility
- The plants in a rain garden should be selected based on their ability to tolerate both wet and dry conditions, their rooting depth and structure, and their aesthetic and wildlife value

iii. Installation Process
- Begin by identifying a suitable location for the rain garden, such as a low-lying area that receives runoff from a roof, driveway, or other impervious surface
- Conduct a soil test to determine the infiltration rate and texture of the existing soil, and amend the soil as needed to achieve a well-draining, sandy loam mix
- Excavate the rain garden to the desired depth and shape, creating a flat bottom and gently sloping sides, and use the excavated soil to create a berm or border around the edges of the garden
- Install an overflow or underdrain system, if needed, to allow excess water to safely exit the rain garden during heavy rainfall events

- Plant the rain garden with a variety of native plants, grasses, and shrubs, using a diverse mix of species and planting densities to create a natural, self-sustaining ecosystem

iv. Maintenance Requirements
- Water the rain garden regularly during the first growing season to help the plants establish deep, healthy root systems
- Remove any weeds or invasive species that may compete with the desired plants, and replace any dead or struggling plants as needed
- Apply a layer of organic mulch around the plants to help retain moisture, suppress weeds, and regulate soil temperature
- Remove any accumulated sediment or debris from the rain garden, particularly after heavy rainfall events, to maintain its infiltration capacity and prevent clogging
- Prune and maintain the plants as needed to promote healthy growth and maintain the desired size and shape of the rain garden

b. Bioswales
i. Definition and Function
- A bioswale is a linear, vegetated channel that is designed to convey, filter, and infiltrate stormwater runoff from roads, parking lots, and other large impervious surfaces
- Bioswales are typically longer and narrower than rain gardens, with a gentle slope that allows water to flow slowly through the channel while being filtered by the plants and soil

- The plants in a bioswale help to slow down the water flow, trap sediment and pollutants, and promote infiltration, while the soil and gravel layers help to filter the water and promote groundwater recharge

ii. Design Considerations
- The size and shape of a bioswale should be based on the size of the contributing drainage area, the expected water flow rate and volume, and the soil type and infiltration rate
- A typical bioswale is sized to convey the peak flow rate from a 10-year storm event, with a maximum flow velocity of 1 foot per second to prevent erosion and allow for adequate filtration and infiltration
- The slope of a bioswale should be between 1% and 6%, with a parabolic or trapezoidal cross-section that allows for even distribution and flow of water
- The soil in a bioswale should be a well-draining, sandy loam mix that is amended with compost or other organic matter to improve its structure and fertility
- The plants in a bioswale should be selected based on their ability to tolerate both wet and dry conditions, their rooting depth and structure, and their ability to filter pollutants and trap sediment

iii. Installation Process
- Begin by identifying a suitable location for the bioswale, such as along a road, parking lot, or other large impervious surface that generates significant stormwater runoff
- Conduct a soil test to determine the infiltration rate and texture of the existing soil, and amend the soil as needed to achieve a well-draining, sandy loam mix

- Excavate the bioswale to the desired depth and shape, creating a parabolic or trapezoidal cross-section with a gentle slope and a flat bottom
- Install an underdrain system, if needed, to allow excess water to safely exit the bioswale during heavy rainfall events
- Plant the bioswale with a variety of native grasses, sedges, and rushes that are adapted to the local climate and soil conditions and that have deep, fibrous root systems

iv. Maintenance Requirements

- Water the bioswale regularly during the first growing season to help the plants establish deep, healthy root systems
- Remove any weeds or invasive species that may compete with the desired plants, and replace any dead or struggling plants as needed
- Mow the vegetation in the bioswale periodically to maintain a height of 6 to 12 inches and prevent the establishment of woody vegetation
- Remove any accumulated sediment or debris from the bioswale, particularly after heavy rainfall events, to maintain its conveyance capacity and prevent clogging
- Inspect the bioswale regularly for signs of erosion, channelization, or other damage, and repair as needed to maintain its function and performance

By incorporating rain gardens and bioswales into your yard's landscaping and drainage plan, you can effectively manage stormwater runoff, reduce the burden on local drainage systems, and create a more sustainable and resilient landscape.

These techniques not only improve the function and efficiency of your yard's drainage system, but also provide valuable ecosystem services, such as water filtration, habitat creation, and aesthetic enhancement. With proper design, installation, and maintenance, rain gardens and bioswales can be an attractive and effective solution for improving drainage and water quality in your yard and beyond.

Permeable Pavers and Porous Surfaces

Permeable pavers and porous surfaces are landscaping techniques that allow stormwater to infiltrate through the surface and into the underlying soil, reducing runoff and promoting groundwater recharge. These techniques use specialized materials and installation methods to create a durable and attractive surface that is both functional and environmentally friendly. In this section, we'll explore permeable pavers and porous surfaces in detail, including their types, benefits, design considerations, installation process, and maintenance requirements.

a. Types of Permeable Pavers and Porous Surfaces
  i. Permeable Interlocking Concrete Pavers (PICP)
- PICPs are a type of paving system that consists of solid concrete pavers with gaps or openings between them that allow water to flow through and into the underlying aggregate layers
- The pavers are typically made from high-strength, durable concrete and are available in a variety of shapes, sizes, and colors to suit different design preferences and applications
- PICPs are suitable for a wide range of applications, including driveways, parking lots, walkways, and patios, and can support heavy loads and traffic
  ii. Porous Asphalt
- Porous asphalt is a type of asphalt pavement that is designed to allow water to flow through the surface and into the underlying aggregate layers

- The asphalt mix is typically made with a higher percentage of air voids and a smaller percentage of fine aggregates than traditional asphalt, which allows water to pass through more easily
- Porous asphalt is suitable for a variety of applications, including parking lots, roads, and trails, and can provide a smoother and quieter surface than traditional asphalt

iii. Pervious Concrete
- Pervious concrete is a type of concrete pavement that is designed to allow water to flow through the surface and into the underlying aggregate layers
- The concrete mix is typically made with a higher percentage of coarse aggregates and a lower percentage of fine aggregates than traditional concrete, which creates a porous structure that allows water to pass through
- Pervious concrete is suitable for a variety of applications, including sidewalks, driveways, and parking lots, and can provide a durable and attractive surface that is resistant to freeze-thaw damage

iv. Grass Pavers
- Grass pavers are a type of paving system that consists of a grid or lattice of concrete or plastic cells that are filled with soil and planted with grass or other vegetation
- The cells provide structural support for the grass and allow water to flow through and into the underlying soil, while the grass helps to filter pollutants and reduce the heat island effect
- Grass pavers are suitable for a variety of applications, including overflow parking areas, emergency access lanes, and recreational trails, and can provide a natural and aesthetically pleasing surface

b. Benefits of Permeable Pavers and Porous Surfaces

i. Reduced Stormwater Runoff
- By allowing water to infiltrate through the surface and into the underlying soil, permeable pavers and porous surfaces can significantly reduce the volume and velocity of stormwater runoff leaving a site
- This can help to reduce the burden on local drainage systems, prevent flooding and erosion, and improve the quality of receiving waters

ii. Improved Water Quality
- As water flows through the permeable surface and underlying aggregate layers, pollutants such as sediment, nutrients, and heavy metals can be filtered out and trapped in the soil
- This can help to improve the quality of the water that eventually reaches local water bodies, and can also help to recharge groundwater aquifers with clean, filtered water

iii. Reduced Heat Island Effect
- Traditional paved surfaces, such as asphalt and concrete, can absorb and retain heat from the sun, contributing to the urban heat island effect and increasing energy costs for cooling
- Permeable pavers and porous surfaces, on the other hand, can help to reduce the heat island effect by allowing water to evaporate from the surface and underlying layers, providing a cooling effect

iv. Enhanced Aesthetics and Functionality
- Permeable pavers and porous surfaces can provide an attractive and functional alternative to traditional paving materials, with a variety of colors, textures, and patterns available to suit different design preferences

- These surfaces can also help to reduce the need for additional drainage infrastructure, such as catch basins and pipes, which can be unsightly and costly to install and maintain

c. Design Considerations for Permeable Pavers and Porous Surfaces

i. Site Suitability
- Permeable pavers and porous surfaces are best suited for sites with well-draining soils and relatively flat slopes (less than 5%)
- Sites with high water tables, shallow bedrock, or contaminated soils may not be suitable for these techniques, as they can limit the infiltration capacity and pose risks to groundwater quality

ii. Drainage Area and Runoff Volume
- The size and design of the permeable surface should be based on the size of the contributing drainage area and the expected runoff volume
- A typical permeable surface is designed to capture and infiltrate the first inch of rainfall from the contributing drainage area, which accounts for the majority of rainfall events in most regions

iii. Subgrade Preparation
- The subgrade (the layer of soil beneath the permeable surface) should be properly prepared to ensure adequate infiltration and structural support
- This may involve excavating and replacing the existing soil with a well-draining, engineered soil mix, and compacting the subgrade to the appropriate density and slope

iv. Aggregate Layers and Geotextiles
- The permeable surface should be underlain by one or more layers of open-graded aggregate (such as gravel or crushed stone) to provide storage and filtration of the infiltrated water
- A layer of geotextile fabric may also be used to separate the aggregate layers from the subgrade and prevent the migration of fine particles into the permeable surface

v. Edge Restraints and Drainage
- The permeable surface should be properly restrained at the edges to prevent shifting and unraveling of the pavers or aggregates
- This may involve installing a concrete curb or edge restraint around the perimeter of the surface, or using a geogrid or other reinforcement material to stabilize the aggregates
- The permeable surface should also be designed with appropriate drainage features, such as underdrains or overflow inlets, to safely convey excess water from the surface and prevent ponding or flooding

d. Installation Process for Permeable Pavers and Porous Surfaces

i. Site Preparation
- Begin by clearing and grading the site to the desired slope and elevation, and removing any existing vegetation, debris, or unsuitable soils
- Excavate the area to the appropriate depth based on the thickness of the permeable surface and underlying aggregate layers, and compact the subgrade to the appropriate density

ii. Subbase Installation
- Install the subbase layer (typically a well-graded, compacted aggregate) to the appropriate depth and slope, and compact it to the appropriate density
- Place a layer of geotextile fabric over the subbase, if specified, to prevent the migration of fine particles into the permeable surface

iii. Base Installation
- Install the base layer (typically an open-graded aggregate) to the appropriate depth and slope, and compact it to the appropriate density
- Place a layer of bedding material (such as sand or fine gravel) over the base, if specified, to provide a smooth and level surface for the pavers or aggregates

iv. Surface Installation
- Install the permeable pavers or porous surface material according to the manufacturer's specifications and industry standards
- For PICPs, place the pavers in the desired pattern and fill the joints with a permeable aggregate or polymeric sand
- For porous asphalt or pervious concrete, place and compact the material in lifts to the appropriate thickness and density, and finish the surface to the desired texture and slope
- For grass pavers, fill the cells with a suitable soil mix and plant the desired vegetation, and water and maintain the surface until the vegetation is established

v. Edge Restraint and Drainage Installation
- Install the edge restraints or drainage features as specified in the design, using appropriate materials and construction techniques

- Ensure that the edge restraints are properly anchored and sealed, and that the drainage features are properly connected and sized to handle the expected water flows

e. Maintenance Requirements for Permeable Pavers and Porous Surfaces

i. Routine Inspection and Cleaning
- Regularly inspect the permeable surface for signs of clogging, damage, or deterioration, such as ponding water, weed growth, or broken pavers
- Remove any debris, sediment, or vegetation from the surface using a broom, leaf blower, or vacuum, taking care not to damage the surface or dislodge the aggregates

ii. Pressure Washing and Vacuuming
- Periodically pressure wash or vacuum the permeable surface to remove accumulated dirt, oil, and other pollutants that can clog the pores and reduce infiltration capacity
- Use a low-pressure, high-volume washing method and a specialized vacuum or regenerative air sweeper to avoid damaging the surface or forcing pollutants into the underlying layers

iii. Joint Filling and Sealing
- For PICPs, periodically refill the joints with permeable aggregate or polymeric sand to maintain the structural integrity and permeability of the surface
- For porous asphalt or pervious concrete, periodically apply a sealant or rejuvenator to the surface to prevent raveling and maintain the porosity and durability of the material

iv. Winter Maintenance
- Avoid using sand, salt, or other deicing chemicals on permeable surfaces, as they can clog the pores and reduce infiltration capacity
- Use physical snow and ice removal methods, such as plowing or shoveling, to maintain the surface during winter months, taking care not to damage the surface or dislodge the aggregates

v. Remediation and Replacement
- If the permeable surface becomes severely clogged or damaged, it may need to be remediated or replaced to restore its infiltration capacity and structural integrity
- This may involve removing and replacing the surface material and underlying aggregates, and repairing or reconstructing the subgrade and drainage features as needed

By incorporating permeable pavers and porous surfaces into your yard's landscaping and drainage plan, you can effectively manage stormwater runoff, improve water quality, reduce the heat island effect, and enhance the aesthetics and functionality of your outdoor spaces. With proper design, installation, and maintenance, these techniques can provide a sustainable and cost-effective solution for improving drainage and water management in your yard and beyond.

Terracing and Retaining Walls

Terracing and retaining walls are landscaping techniques used to manage steep slopes, prevent soil erosion, and create usable, level spaces in yards with challenging topography. These techniques involve the construction of structures that hold back soil and create a series of stepped or terraced levels, allowing for better drainage, easier maintenance, and more functional outdoor living areas. In this section, we'll explore terracing and retaining walls in detail, including their benefits, design considerations, materials, installation process, and maintenance requirements.

a. Benefits of Terracing and Retaining Walls
 i. Slope Stabilization and Erosion Control
- Terracing and retaining walls help to stabilize steep slopes by holding back soil and reducing the angle of the slope
- This can help to prevent soil erosion, landslides, and other slope failures that can damage property and pose safety hazards

 ii. Improved Drainage and Water Management
- By creating level terraces or steps, terracing and retaining walls can help to slow down and redirect water flow, reducing runoff and promoting infiltration
- This can help to prevent water from pooling or eroding the soil, and can also help to distribute water more evenly across the landscape

 iii. Increased Usable Space and Accessibility
- Terracing and retaining walls can create level, usable spaces on steep slopes that would otherwise be difficult or impossible to access or maintain

- This can allow for the creation of garden beds, patios, walkways, and other outdoor living areas that can enhance the functionality and enjoyment of the yard

iv. Enhanced Aesthetics and Property Value
- Well-designed and constructed terracing and retaining walls can add visual interest, texture, and depth to the landscape, creating a more attractive and dynamic outdoor space
- These features can also increase the value and appeal of the property, particularly in areas with challenging topography or limited usable space

b. Design Considerations for Terracing and Retaining Walls

i. Site Assessment and Soil Analysis
- Before designing terracing or retaining walls, it's important to assess the site conditions, including the slope, soil type, and drainage patterns
- A soil analysis can help to determine the bearing capacity, compaction, and permeability of the soil, which can inform the design and construction of the walls

ii. Wall Height and Placement
- The height and placement of the retaining walls should be based on the slope and grade of the site, as well as the desired level of terracing and usable space
- Walls that are too tall or too close together can create drainage and maintenance issues, while walls that are too short or too far apart may not provide adequate stabilization or usable space

iii. Drainage and Waterproofing
- Proper drainage and waterproofing are critical for the long-term performance and stability of terracing and retaining walls
- This may involve the installation of drainage pipes, weep holes, or other drainage features behind the walls, as well as the use of waterproofing membranes or coatings to prevent water infiltration and damage

iv. Material Selection and Aesthetics
- Retaining walls can be constructed from a variety of materials, including concrete, stone, brick, wood, or gabions (wire cages filled with rock)
- The choice of material should be based on factors such as the desired aesthetic, durability, cost, and site conditions
- The color, texture, and pattern of the materials should be selected to complement the surrounding landscape and architecture

c. Installation Process for Terracing and Retaining Walls

i. Site Preparation and Excavation
- Begin by clearing and grading the site to the desired slope and elevation, and removing any existing vegetation, debris, or unsuitable soils
- Excavate the area behind the proposed wall location to the appropriate depth and width, based on the size and type of wall being installed

ii. Foundation Preparation
- Install a level and stable foundation for the retaining wall, typically consisting of compacted gravel or concrete
- The foundation should be deep enough to extend below the frost line and wide enough to support the weight and size of the wall

iii. Drainage Installation
- Install any necessary drainage features behind the wall, such as perforated pipes, weep holes, or drainage boards
- The drainage system should be designed to collect and redirect water away from the wall and prevent hydrostatic pressure from building up behind the wall

iv. Wall Construction
- Construct the retaining wall using the selected materials and construction techniques, following the manufacturer's specifications and local building codes
- For segmental block walls, stack the blocks in a staggered pattern and use pins or clips to secure them together
- For poured concrete walls, build forms and pour the concrete in lifts, using rebar or other reinforcement as needed
- For other types of walls, such as stone or wood, follow the appropriate construction methods and best practices for the material

v. Backfilling and Compaction
- Backfill the area behind the wall with a free-draining, granular material, such as gravel or crushed stone
- Compact the backfill in lifts to the appropriate density, taking care not to damage the drainage system or apply excessive pressure to the wall

vi. Finishing and Landscaping
- Install any necessary caps, coping, or other finishing elements on top of the wall to protect it from water and provide a finished appearance

- Grade and landscape the area around the wall and terraces, using appropriate plantings, mulches, and other materials to enhance the aesthetic and functionality of the space

d. Maintenance Requirements for Terracing and Retaining Walls

i. Regular Inspection and Monitoring
- Regularly inspect the terracing and retaining walls for signs of damage, settlement, or instability, such as cracks, bulges, or leaning
- Monitor the drainage system to ensure that it is functioning properly and not clogged or damaged

ii. Drainage Maintenance
- Periodically clean out the drainage pipes, weep holes, or other drainage features to remove any accumulated sediment or debris
- Repair or replace any damaged or clogged drainage components to maintain the effectiveness of the system

iii. Wall Repair and Repointing
- Repair any cracks, spalls, or other damage to the retaining wall using appropriate patching or sealing materials
- For masonry walls, periodically repoint the joints between the units using a compatible mortar or grout to maintain the structural integrity and appearance of the wall

iv. Vegetation Management
- Manage the vegetation on and around the terracing and retaining walls to prevent damage from roots, vines, or other growth

- Prune or remove any trees or large shrubs that may compromise the stability of the walls, and avoid planting species with aggressive root systems near the walls

v. Erosion Control and Slope Stabilization
- Monitor the slopes and soil around the terracing and retaining walls for signs of erosion, slumping, or instability
- Implement erosion control measures, such as planting groundcovers, installing erosion control blankets, or applying mulch, to prevent soil loss and maintain the stability of the slopes

By incorporating terracing and retaining walls into your yard's landscaping and drainage plan, you can effectively manage steep slopes, prevent soil erosion, and create usable, level spaces that enhance the functionality and aesthetic of your outdoor living areas. With proper design, installation, and maintenance, these techniques can provide a long-lasting and attractive solution for improving drainage and slope stability in your yard, while also adding value and appeal to your property.

Planting Strategies for Better Drainage

Proper plant selection and placement can play a significant role in improving drainage and managing water in your yard. By choosing plants that are well-suited to the soil conditions and moisture levels in your landscape, and by arranging them in a way that promotes good drainage and water uptake, you can create a more resilient and sustainable yard that is better able to handle excess water and prevent drainage issues. In this section, we'll explore planting strategies for better drainage, including plant selection, placement, and maintenance considerations.

a. Plant Selection for Drainage
  i. Native and Adapted Plants
- Choose plants that are native or well-adapted to your region and climate, as they are more likely to be tolerant of the local soil and moisture conditions
- Native plants often have deep, extensive root systems that can help to improve soil structure, increase infiltration, and reduce runoff

  ii. Moisture-Tolerant Plants
- In areas of your yard that are prone to poor drainage or standing water, choose plants that are tolerant of wet or saturated soil conditions
- Examples of moisture-tolerant plants include sedges, rushes, ferns, and certain perennials and shrubs

  iii. Drought-Tolerant Plants
- In areas of your yard that are prone to dry or well-drained soil conditions, choose plants that are tolerant of drought or low moisture levels

- Examples of drought-tolerant plants include succulents, ornamental grasses, and certain perennials and shrubs

iv. Deep-Rooted Plants
- Choose plants with deep, fibrous root systems that can help to break up compacted soil, improve infiltration, and increase the soil's water-holding capacity
- Examples of deep-rooted plants include prairie grasses, legumes, and certain trees and shrubs

b. Plant Placement for Drainage

i. Grading and Contouring
- Use plants to help control and direct the flow of water in your yard by placing them strategically in relation to the grading and contouring of the landscape
- Place moisture-tolerant plants in low-lying areas or swales where water tends to collect, and place drought-tolerant plants on higher ground or slopes where water tends to drain away

ii. Layering and Grouping
- Use a layered approach to planting, with taller trees and shrubs at the back, followed by shorter perennials and groundcovers in front
- Group plants with similar water needs together to create hydrozones, or areas of the landscape with similar irrigation requirements

iii. Spacing and Density
- Plant trees, shrubs, and perennials at an appropriate spacing and density to allow for good air circulation and prevent overcrowding, which can lead to poor drainage and disease issues

- Consider the mature size and growth habit of the plants when determining spacing, and allow enough room for them to grow and spread over time

iv. Drainage and Infiltration
- Use plants to help improve drainage and infiltration in your yard by placing them in areas where water tends to pool or run off
- Create rain gardens or bioswales planted with deep-rooted, moisture-tolerant species to capture and filter stormwater runoff, and use vegetated buffer strips along paths and driveways to slow down and absorb water

c. Plant Maintenance for Drainage

i. Watering and Irrigation
- Water plants deeply and infrequently to encourage deep root growth and improve the soil's water-holding capacity
- Use drip irrigation or soaker hoses to deliver water directly to the plant roots, and avoid overhead sprinklers that can lead to runoff and evaporation

ii. Mulching and Soil Amendment
- Apply a layer of organic mulch around plants to help retain moisture, suppress weeds, and improve soil structure and fertility
- Amend the soil with compost, leaf mold, or other organic matter to improve its texture, drainage, and water-holding capacity

iii. Pruning and Thinning
- Prune trees and shrubs regularly to remove dead, diseased, or crossing branches, and to promote good air circulation and light penetration

- Thin out dense growth or overgrown areas to improve drainage and prevent water from pooling or standing in the landscape

iv. Weed and Pest Management
- Control weeds and invasive plants that can compete with desirable vegetation for water and nutrients, and create drainage issues by clogging up waterways or soil pores
- Monitor plants for signs of pests or disease, and use integrated pest management (IPM) strategies to address any issues that arise, such as using beneficial insects or targeted sprays

d. Case Studies and Examples

i. Rain Garden Design
- A homeowner in a suburban neighborhood creates a rain garden in a low-lying area of their front yard to capture and filter stormwater runoff from their roof and driveway
- The rain garden is planted with a mix of native perennials, grasses, and shrubs that are adapted to the local climate and soil conditions, and can tolerate both wet and dry periods
- The rain garden helps to reduce runoff and improve water quality, while also providing habitat for pollinators and other wildlife

ii. Slope Stabilization with Groundcovers
- A property owner with a steep, eroding hillside in their backyard uses a combination of terracing, retaining walls, and groundcover plantings to stabilize the slope and improve drainage

- The groundcovers, which include a mix of low-growing perennials and grasses, help to hold the soil in place, slow down water flow, and promote infiltration
- The terracing and retaining walls create level planting areas and prevent soil erosion, while also providing a visually interesting and functional landscape feature

iii. Xeriscape Conversion

- A homeowner in a dry, arid climate decides to convert their traditional, high-water-use landscape into a xeriscape, or low-water-use landscape
- The xeriscape includes a mix of drought-tolerant native and adapted plants, such as succulents, cacti, and ornamental grasses, as well as hardscape features like gravel mulch and boulder accents
- The xeriscape helps to reduce water use and improve drainage, while also creating a unique and sustainable landscape that is well-suited to the local environment

By incorporating planting strategies for better drainage into your yard's landscaping and water management plan, you can create a more resilient, sustainable, and visually appealing outdoor space. By selecting plants that are well-adapted to your local climate and soil conditions, placing them strategically in relation to the grading and drainage patterns of your yard, and maintaining them properly over time, you can effectively manage excess water, prevent drainage issues, and support a healthy and thriving landscape. Whether you are dealing with a small urban lot or a large rural property, there are many ways to use plants to improve drainage and create a more functional and attractive yard.

Maintaining Your Drainage-Friendly Landscape

Creating a drainage-friendly landscape is an important step in managing water flow and preventing issues like erosion, standing water, and property damage. However, to ensure that your landscape continues to function effectively and look its best over time, regular maintenance is essential. In this section, we'll explore the key aspects of maintaining a drainage-friendly landscape, including inspections, cleaning and repairs, plant care, and troubleshooting common issues.

a. Regular Inspections and Monitoring
   i. Drainage Systems
- Regularly inspect your yard's drainage systems, such as gutters, downspouts, French drains, and catch basins, to ensure that they are functioning properly and not clogged or damaged
- Look for signs of wear, corrosion, or leaks, and make repairs or replacements as needed to prevent water from backing up or overflowing

   ii. Soil and Grading
- Monitor the soil and grading in your yard for signs of erosion, settling, or unevenness, which can indicate drainage problems or other issues
- Check for areas where water is pooling or running off instead of infiltrating, and take steps to correct the grading or improve the soil structure as needed

iii. Plants and Vegetation
- Observe the health and growth of your plants and vegetation, looking for signs of stress, disease, or damage that could be related to poor drainage or overwatering
- Monitor trees and shrubs for root problems or invasive growth that could be blocking or damaging drainage systems, and take corrective action as needed

b. Cleaning and Repairs
i. Debris Removal
- Regularly remove debris like leaves, twigs, and litter from your yard's drainage systems and landscaped areas to prevent clogs and blockages
- Use a hose, rake, or other tool to clear out gutters, downspouts, and catch basins, and dispose of the debris properly

ii. Sediment and Silt Removal
- Over time, sediment and silt can build up in drainage systems and low-lying areas, reducing their capacity and effectiveness
- Use a shovel, trowel, or other tool to remove excess sediment and silt from French drains, swales, and other drainage features, and dispose of it away from the area

iii. Erosion Control and Repair
- Address any areas of erosion or soil loss promptly to prevent further damage and maintain the integrity of your landscape
- Use erosion control measures like mulch, ground covers, or erosion control blankets to stabilize the soil and prevent further loss, and repair any damaged areas with fresh soil or plantings

iv. Hardscape Maintenance and Repair
- Regularly inspect and maintain hardscape features like retaining walls, terraces, and permeable pavers to ensure that they are stable, level, and functioning properly
- Make repairs or replacements as needed to address any cracks, settling, or other damage, and keep the surfaces clean and free of debris

c. **Plant Care and Management**
i. Watering and Irrigation
- Adjust your watering and irrigation practices to ensure that your plants are getting the right amount of moisture for their needs and the conditions in your yard
- Avoid overwatering, which can lead to drainage problems and plant health issues, and use efficient irrigation methods like drip irrigation or soaker hoses to minimize runoff and evaporation

ii. Pruning and Trimming
- Regularly prune and trim your trees, shrubs, and perennials to maintain their shape, size, and health, and to prevent overgrowth or invasive roots from blocking or damaging drainage systems
- Remove any dead, diseased, or damaged branches or foliage, and dispose of the debris properly to prevent the spread of pests or diseases

iii. Mulching and Soil Amendment
- Apply a layer of organic mulch around your plants and in landscaped areas to help retain moisture, suppress weeds, and improve soil structure and fertility

- Amend the soil with compost, leaf mold, or other organic matter as needed to improve its texture, drainage, and water-holding capacity, and to support healthy plant growth

iv. Weed and Pest Management
- Monitor your landscape for signs of weeds, pests, or diseases that could be impacting the health and appearance of your plants or the functioning of your drainage systems
- Use integrated pest management (IPM) strategies to address any issues that arise, such as hand-pulling weeds, using beneficial insects, or applying targeted treatments as needed

d. Troubleshooting Common Issues
i. Standing Water and Ponding
- If you notice areas of standing water or ponding in your yard, even after a rain event has ended, it could indicate a drainage problem or other issue
- Check for clogs or blockages in your drainage systems, and clear them out as needed to restore proper flow and infiltration
- Consider adding additional drainage features like French drains, swales, or catch basins to help move water away from problem areas and prevent ponding

ii. Soil Erosion and Washouts
- If you notice areas of soil erosion or washouts in your yard, especially after heavy rain or storm events, it could indicate a problem with your grading, drainage, or soil structure

- Use erosion control measures like mulch, ground covers, or erosion control blankets to stabilize the soil and prevent further loss
- Consider adding retaining walls, terraces, or other hardscape features to help control water flow and prevent erosion in steep or sloped areas

iii. Plant Stress and Dieback
- If you notice your plants showing signs of stress, wilting, or dieback, especially in areas with poor drainage or overwatering, it could indicate a problem with your soil or irrigation practices
- Check the soil moisture levels and adjust your watering schedule as needed to ensure that your plants are getting the right amount of water for their needs
- Consider adding drainage features like French drains or permeable pavers to help improve soil moisture levels and prevent waterlogging

iv. Drainage System Failures
- If you notice your drainage systems failing or not functioning properly, such as gutters overflowing, French drains clogging, or catch basins filling up, it could indicate a problem with the design, installation, or maintenance of the system
- Inspect the system for clogs, leaks, or damage, and make repairs or replacements as needed to restore proper function and flow
- Consider hiring a professional landscaper or drainage specialist to assess the system and recommend any necessary upgrades or modifications to improve performance and reliability

Chapter 4
Preventing Water Damage in Your Home

Gutter and Downspout Maintenance

Gutters and downspouts play a crucial role in protecting your home from water damage by collecting and directing rainwater away from your foundation, walls, and landscaping. However, when gutters and downspouts become clogged, damaged, or improperly installed, they can actually contribute to water damage by allowing water to overflow, leak, or pool around your home. In this section, we'll explore the importance of gutter and downspout maintenance, and provide tips and best practices for keeping your gutters and downspouts functioning effectively.

a. The Importance of Gutter and Downspout Maintenance
  i. Preventing Water Damage
- Clogged or damaged gutters and downspouts can allow water to overflow or leak, leading to a range of water damage issues like foundation cracks, basement flooding, and soil erosion
- Regular gutter and downspout maintenance can help prevent these issues by ensuring that water is properly collected and directed away from your home and foundation

  ii. Protecting Your Home's Structure
- When gutters and downspouts fail to function properly, water can seep into your home's walls, roof, and foundation, causing structural damage like rot, mold, and deterioration

- Maintaining your gutters and downspouts can help protect your home's structure by keeping water away from vulnerable areas and preventing moisture buildup

iii. Extending the Life of Your Roof
- Clogged gutters can cause water to back up and overflow onto your roof, leading to leaks, damage, and premature aging of your roofing materials
- By keeping your gutters clear and free-flowing, you can help extend the life of your roof and avoid costly repairs or replacements

iv. Maintaining Your Home's Value and Appearance
- Neglected gutters and downspouts can detract from your home's curb appeal and overall value, as well as create unsightly stains, streaks, and damage to your exterior walls and landscaping
- Regular gutter and downspout maintenance can help maintain your home's appearance and value, and prevent the need for expensive cosmetic repairs or replacements

b. Gutter and Downspout Cleaning

i. Frequency and Timing
- Gutters and downspouts should be cleaned at least twice a year, typically in the spring and fall, to remove accumulated debris and ensure proper water flow
- More frequent cleaning may be necessary if your home is surrounded by trees or in an area with heavy rainfall or storms

ii. Safety Precautions
- Gutter and downspout cleaning can be dangerous, as it often involves working on ladders or roofs at high heights

- Always use proper safety equipment like gloves, eye protection, and sturdy ladders, and avoid reaching or overexerting yourself
- Consider hiring a professional gutter cleaning service if you are uncomfortable or unable to perform the work safely yourself

iii. Tools and Techniques
- Use a sturdy ladder, bucket, and gutter scoop or trowel to remove debris from your gutters, starting at the downspout and working your way toward the end
- Use a garden hose to flush out any remaining debris and check for proper water flow, and use a plumber's snake or auger to clear any clogs in the downspouts
- Use a gutter brush or vacuum attachment to clean the inside of your gutters, and use a pressure washer or cleaning solution to remove any stains or buildup on the exterior

iv. Disposal of Debris
- Collect the debris removed from your gutters in a bucket or bag, and dispose of it in your yard waste or compost bin
- Avoid leaving debris on your roof, landscaping, or near your foundation, as it can attract pests, hold moisture, and contribute to future clogs or damage

c. Gutter and Downspout Repairs and Maintenance

i. Identifying Damage and Leaks
- Regularly inspect your gutters and downspouts for signs of damage, leaks, or improper function, such as cracks, holes, rust, sagging, or overflowing water

- Check for signs of water damage or staining on your walls, foundation, or landscaping, which can indicate a problem with your gutter or downspout system

ii. Repairing Leaks and Holes
- Use a gutter sealant or patch kit to repair small leaks or holes in your gutters or downspouts, following the manufacturer's instructions for application and curing
- For larger or more extensive damage, consider replacing the affected section of gutter or downspout with a new piece that matches the existing material and profile

iii. Adjusting Pitch and Alignment
- Check the pitch and alignment of your gutters and downspouts to ensure that water is flowing properly and not pooling or overflowing
- Adjust the pitch of your gutters to ensure a slight slope towards the downspouts (about 1/4 inch per 10 feet of gutter), using a level and adjustable gutter hangers or brackets
- Adjust the alignment of your downspouts to ensure that they are directing water at least 4-5 feet away from your foundation, using downspout extensions or splash blocks as needed

iv. Tightening and Securing Connections
- Check the connections between your gutters, downspouts, and fascia board to ensure that they are tight, secure, and not leaking or coming loose
- Use gutter screws, brackets, or hangers to secure any loose or sagging sections, and use a caulking gun or sealant to seal any gaps or leaks at the connections

v. Replacing Damaged or Aging Components
- If your gutters or downspouts are extensively damaged, rusted, or aging, consider replacing them with new components that match the style and material of your home
- Choose high-quality, durable materials like aluminum, copper, or steel, and look for features like seamless construction, leaf guards, and covered downspouts to improve performance and longevity
- Hire a professional gutter installation company to ensure proper sizing, pitch, and installation of your new gutter and downspout system

d. **Preventing Future Clogs and Damage**
i. Installing Gutter Guards or Covers
- Consider installing gutter guards, covers, or screens over your gutters to prevent leaves, twigs, and other debris from accumulating and causing clogs
- Choose a gutter guard system that matches the style and material of your gutters, and look for features like fine mesh screens, reverse curves, or micro-mesh filters to maximize protection and water flow

ii. Trimming Nearby Trees and Vegetation
- Regularly trim any trees, shrubs, or vegetation that overhang or grow near your gutters and downspouts to reduce the amount of debris that falls into them
- Use a pole saw, pruning shears, or professional tree trimming service to remove any branches or limbs that are within a few feet of your gutters or roof

iii. Maintaining Proper Landscaping and Grading
- Ensure that your landscaping and grading are properly designed and maintained to direct water away from your foundation and prevent it from pooling or eroding near your downspouts
- Use downspout extensions, splash blocks, or underground drainage systems to direct water at least 4-5 feet away from your foundation, and ensure that the soil slopes away from your home at a rate of at least 6 inches per 10 feet

iv. Conducting Regular Inspections and Maintenance
- Establish a regular schedule for inspecting and maintaining your gutters, downspouts, and surrounding landscaping to identify and address any issues before they cause damage or costly repairs
- Keep a record of your maintenance tasks and observations, and consider hiring a professional gutter and landscaping service for more complex or time-consuming tasks

By following these gutter and downspout maintenance practices and tips, you can help protect your home from water damage, maintain your home's value and appearance, and extend the life of your roof and other structural components. Regular cleaning, repairs, and preventative measures can go a long way toward ensuring that your gutters and downspouts are functioning effectively and efficiently, and can save you time, money, and stress in the long run.

Foundation Waterproofing and Grading

Proper foundation waterproofing and grading are essential for preventing water damage to your home's structure and interior. When water is allowed to seep into or pool around your foundation, it can lead to a range of serious problems like cracks, leaks, settling, and mold growth. In this section, we'll explore the importance of foundation waterproofing and grading, and provide tips and best practices for keeping your home dry, stable, and protected from water damage.

a. The Importance of Foundation Waterproofing and Grading

i. Preventing Water Infiltration

- Foundation waterproofing creates a barrier that prevents water from seeping through your foundation walls and floor, helping to keep your basement or crawl space dry and free from moisture-related issues
- Proper grading ensures that water flows away from your foundation and does not pool or collect near your home, reducing the risk of hydrostatic pressure and water infiltration

ii. Maintaining Structural Integrity

- When water is allowed to penetrate or pool around your foundation, it can cause the soil to expand, shift, or erode, leading to cracks, settling, or other structural damage
- Foundation waterproofing and grading help to maintain the stability and integrity of your home's structure by keeping water away from your foundation and preventing soil-related issues

iii. Protecting Your Home's Value and Livability
- Water damage to your foundation and interior can be costly to repair and can significantly impact your home's value, appearance, and livability
- Proper foundation waterproofing and grading can help protect your home from water-related issues like mold, rot, and pest infestations, and can save you money and stress in the long run

iv. Meeting Building Codes and Regulations
- Most local building codes and regulations require homes to have proper foundation waterproofing and grading to ensure the safety, health, and longevity of the structure
- Failing to meet these requirements can result in fines, legal issues, or difficulty selling your home in the future

b. Foundation Waterproofing Techniques

i. Exterior Waterproofing
- Exterior waterproofing involves excavating the soil around your foundation and applying a waterproof membrane or coating to the exterior walls
- Common waterproofing materials include asphalt-based coatings, rubber membranes, and bentonite clay, which are applied in layers and sealed with drainage boards or insulation
- Exterior waterproofing is typically recommended for new construction or when there is no existing water damage or interior access to the foundation

ii. Interior Waterproofing
- Interior waterproofing involves applying a waterproof sealant or membrane to the interior walls and floor of your basement or crawl space

- Common waterproofing materials include hydraulic cement, silicate-based sealants, and epoxy injections, which are applied directly to the concrete or masonry surfaces
- Interior waterproofing is typically recommended for existing homes with minor water seepage or when exterior excavation is not feasible or cost-effective

iii. French Drains and Sump Pumps

- French drains are perforated pipes that are installed around the perimeter of your foundation to collect and redirect water away from your home
- Sump pumps are mechanical devices that are installed in a pit in your basement or crawl space to pump out any water that accumulates inside your foundation
- Both French drains and sump pumps are often used in conjunction with other waterproofing techniques to provide additional protection and drainage for your foundation

iv. Foundation Crack Repair

- Foundation cracks can allow water to seep into your basement or crawl space, and can also indicate underlying structural issues that need to be addressed
- Crack repair involves injecting a flexible, waterproof sealant or epoxy into the crack to fill it and prevent water infiltration
- For larger or more severe cracks, additional repairs like carbon fiber reinforcement or steel bracing may be necessary to restore your foundation's strength and stability

c. Proper Grading Techniques

i. Slope and Pitch
- Proper grading involves creating a slope or pitch that directs water away from your foundation and towards a drainage system or natural outletThe ideal slope is
- typically a 6-inch drop over a 10-foot distance (5% grade) for the first 4-6 feet around your foundation, with a more gradual slope beyond that
- Avoid creating low spots, depressions, or flat areas near your foundation where water can pool or collect

ii. Soil Type and Compaction
- The type and compaction of the soil around your foundation can greatly impact its ability to absorb and drain water
- Sandy or gravelly soils tend to drain water more quickly, while clay or silty soils tend to retain water and can expand or shift when wet
- Proper grading involves using well-draining, compacted soil that is free from debris, organic matter, or large rocks that can impede water flow

iii. Drainage Systems and Outlets
- In addition to sloping the soil away from your foundation, it's important to have a drainage system or outlet that can safely carry the water away from your property
- Common drainage systems include French drains, swales, catch basins, and underground pipes that direct water to a storm sewer, pond, or other natural outlet

- Ensure that your drainage system is properly sized, installed, and maintained to handle the expected water volume and flow rate for your area

iv. Landscaping and Vegetation
- Landscaping and vegetation can also play a role in proper grading and drainage around your foundation
- Avoid planting trees, shrubs, or other plants with deep or invasive roots near your foundation, as they can cause damage or blockages to your drainage system
- Use mulch, gravel, or other porous materials around your foundation plantings to allow water to infiltrate and drain more easily
- Consider creating a rain garden or bioswale to capture and filter stormwater runoff from your roof, driveway, or other impervious surfaces

d. Maintaining Your Foundation Waterproofing and Grading

i. Regular Inspections and Monitoring
- Regularly inspect your foundation and grading for signs of water infiltration, cracks, settling, or other issues that could indicate a problem with your waterproofing or drainage
- Monitor your basement or crawl space for moisture, mold, or musty odors, and use a moisture meter or humidity gauge to track the relative humidity levels
- Keep an eye on your sump pump, French drains, and other drainage systems to ensure they are functioning properly and not clogged or damaged

ii. Cleaning and Repairs
- Clean your gutters, downspouts, and drainage systems regularly to remove debris, leaves, and other blockages that can impede water flow
- Repair any cracks, holes, or other damage to your foundation walls or floor promptly to prevent water infiltration and further deterioration
- If you notice any major issues or failures with your waterproofing or grading, contact a professional foundation repair or waterproofing contractor for an assessment and recommendation

iii. Proper Landscaping and Watering Practices
- Avoid overwatering your foundation plantings or allowing sprinklers or hoses to spray directly onto your foundation walls
- Use drought-tolerant, native plants and xeriscaping techniques to reduce the amount of water needed for your landscaping
- Ensure that your downspouts and drainage outlets are directing water at least 4-6 feet away from your foundation, and use splash blocks or extensions to prevent soil erosion

iv. Professional Maintenance and Upgrades
- Consider hiring a professional foundation waterproofing or grading contractor to inspect and maintain your system every few years, or whenever you notice any issues or changes in performance
- If your home is older or has a history of water problems, you may want to consider upgrading your waterproofing or drainage system with newer, more effective technologies or materials

- Some common upgrades include installing a perimeter drain system, adding a backup sump pump or battery, or applying a more durable waterproofing membrane or coating to your foundation walls and floor

By following these foundation waterproofing and grading best practices and maintenance tips, you can help protect your home from water damage, maintain its structural integrity and value, and create a dry, healthy, and comfortable living space. Whether you're building a new home or retrofitting an existing one, investing in proper foundation waterproofing and grading is one of the best ways to safeguard your property and your peace of mind.

Sump Pump Installation and Maintenance

Sump pumps are an essential component of many home waterproofing and drainage systems, particularly in areas with high water tables, frequent flooding, or poor soil drainage. A sump pump is a mechanical device that is installed in a pit (or sump) in your basement or crawl space, and is designed to pump out any water that accumulates inside your foundation, helping to prevent water damage, mold growth, and other moisture-related issues. In this section, we'll explore the basics of sump pump installation and maintenance, and provide tips and best practices for keeping your sump pump functioning effectively and reliably.

a. Sump Pump Basics
  i. Types of Sump Pumps
- Submersible pumps: These pumps are designed to be fully submerged in water and are typically more quiet, efficient, and long-lasting than pedestal pumps. They are also less visible and take up less space in your sump pit.
- Pedestal pumps: These pumps have a motor that sits above the water level on a pedestal, with only the impeller and intake submerged in water. They are typically less expensive and easier to maintain than submersible pumps, but are also louder and less efficient.
- Battery backup pumps: These pumps are designed to operate on battery power in case of a power outage or primary pump failure. They provide an extra layer of protection and peace of mind, particularly in areas with frequent storms or power disruptions.

ii. Sump Pump Components
- Motor: The motor is the heart of the sump pump and provides the power to pump water out of your sump pit and away from your foundation.
- Float switch: The float switch is a device that senses the water level in your sump pit and turns the pump on and off as needed. It ensures that the pump only runs when there is enough water to pump out, and helps to prevent the pump from running dry or burning out.
- Check valve: The check valve is a one-way valve that is installed on the discharge pipe of the pump. It prevents water from flowing back into the sump pit when the pump is not running, and helps to maintain the prime of the pump.
- Discharge pipe: The discharge pipe carries the water from the pump to the outside of your home or to a drainage system. It should be properly sized, sealed, and insulated to prevent leaks, freezing, and other issues.

iii. Sizing and Capacity
- Sump pumps are typically sized based on the horsepower (HP) of the motor and the gallons per minute (GPM) or gallons per hour (GPH) of water that they can pump out.
- The size and capacity of your sump pump will depend on factors like the size of your sump pit, the depth of your basement or crawl space, the amount of water you typically experience, and the distance and height of your discharge pipe.
- As a general rule, a 1/3 HP pump can handle most residential applications, while a 1/2 HP or larger pump may be needed for larger or more severe water problems.

- It's important to choose a pump with enough capacity to handle your expected water volume, but not so much that it cycles on and off too frequently or overwhelms your discharge system.

b. Sump Pump Installation
i. Sump Pit Preparation
- Before installing your sump pump, you'll need to prepare your sump pit by digging a hole in your basement or crawl space floor, typically near the lowest point or where water tends to collect.
- The pit should be at least 2 feet deep and 18 inches wide, with a solid bottom and a perforated or gravel-filled sides to allow water to enter from the surrounding soil.
- If you have an existing sump pit, you may need to clean it out, repair any cracks or damage, and ensure that it is properly sized and located for your new pump.

ii. Pump and Plumbing Installation
- Once your sump pit is prepared, you can install your sump pump by placing it in the center of the pit and connecting it to a power source and discharge pipe.
- For submersible pumps, the pump should be placed on a level, stable base (such as a brick or paver) and the float switch should be positioned to turn the pump on when the water level rises to a predetermined height.
- For pedestal pumps, the motor should be placed on a stable, elevated platform above the water level, with the intake and float switch extending into the sump pit.

- The discharge pipe should be connected to the pump outlet using a check valve and a union or coupling to allow for easy removal and maintenance. The pipe should be routed to the outside of your home, at least 10 feet away from your foundation, and should terminate with a splash block or other erosion-control device.

iii. Electrical and Safety Considerations

- Sump pumps typically require a dedicated electrical circuit and GFCI (ground-fault circuit interrupter) outlet to ensure safe and reliable operation.
- The circuit should be properly sized and grounded, and should be installed by a licensed electrician to meet local building codes and standards.
- The pump should also be equipped with a cover or grate to prevent debris, animals, or children from falling into the sump pit, and should be labeled with warning signs or tags to indicate the presence of electrical and water hazards.

iv. Testing and Monitoring

- After installation, it's important to test your sump pump to ensure that it is working properly and to familiarize yourself with its operation and maintenance needs.
- You can test the pump by manually filling the sump pit with water until the float switch activates the pump, and then monitoring the water level and discharge flow to ensure that the pump is removing water effectively.
- You should also install a water alarm or monitoring system that can alert you if the water level in your sump pit rises above a certain level or if the pump fails to operate when needed.

- Some newer sump pumps also come with Wi-Fi or smartphone connectivity, allowing you to monitor and control the pump remotely and receive alerts or notifications if any issues arise.

c. Sump Pump Maintenance
i. Regular Inspections and Testing
- To keep your sump pump functioning effectively and reliably, it's important to perform regular inspections and testing, at least once a year or more frequently if you live in an area with high water table or frequent flooding.
- During your inspections, you should check the pump for any signs of wear, damage, or corrosion, and ensure that the float switch, check valve, and discharge pipe are working properly and free from obstructions.
- You should also test the pump by manually filling the sump pit with water and observing the pump's operation and discharge flow, as well as testing the water alarm or monitoring system to ensure that it is functioning properly.

ii. Cleaning and Repairs
- Over time, your sump pump may accumulate dirt, debris, or mineral buildup that can affect its performance and longevity.
- To clean the pump, you should unplug it from the power source, remove it from the sump pit, and use a garden hose or soft brush to remove any debris or buildup from the pump housing, impeller, and intake screen.
- If you notice any damage or wear to the pump components, such as a cracked housing, worn impeller, or faulty float switch, you may need to repair or replace those parts to ensure proper operation.

- You should also periodically clean and inspect the sump pit itself, removing any debris or sediment that may have accumulated and ensuring that the perforations or gravel bed are allowing water to enter freely.

iii. Battery Backup Maintenance

- If you have a battery backup sump pump, you'll need to perform additional maintenance to ensure that the battery is charged and ready to operate when needed.
- Most battery backup pumps use a deep-cycle marine battery that should be replaced every 3-5 years or as recommended by the manufacturer.
- You should also periodically test the battery and charging system by unplugging the primary pump and allowing the backup pump to operate on battery power, monitoring the battery voltage and discharge time to ensure that it is sufficient for your needs.
- You may also need to add distilled water to the battery cells periodically to maintain the proper electrolyte level and prevent damage or corrosion.

iv. Professional Maintenance and Upgrades

- While many homeowners can perform basic sump pump maintenance and repairs on their own, there may be times when professional assistance is needed, particularly for more complex or technical issues.
- If you notice any major performance issues, electrical problems, or structural damage to your sump pump or sump pit, it's best to contact a licensed plumber or waterproofing contractor for an assessment and recommendation.

- You may also want to consider upgrading your sump pump or adding additional features or components, such as a battery backup system, high-water alarm, or remote monitoring system, to provide an extra layer of protection and peace of mind.
- A professional can help you evaluate your options and choose the best solution for your specific needs and budget, as well as ensure that any upgrades or modifications are installed and functioning properly.

By following these sump pump installation and maintenance best practices and tips, you can help ensure that your sump pump is working effectively and reliably to protect your home from water damage and moisture-related issues. Whether you're installing a new sump pump or maintaining an existing one, investing in proper care and attention can save you time, money, and stress in the long run, and provide valuable peace of mind for you and your family.

Identifying and Fixing Leaks and Moisture Issues

Leaks and moisture issues are common problems in many homes, and can lead to a range of serious and costly damage if left unchecked. From water stains and musty odors to structural damage and mold growth, the effects of leaks and moisture can be both unsightly and unhealthy, and can significantly impact your home's value, comfort, and safety. In this section, we'll explore the most common types of leaks and moisture issues, and provide tips and best practices for identifying, diagnosing, and fixing these problems to keep your home dry, healthy, and protected.

a. Common Types of Leaks and Moisture Issues
  i. Roof Leaks
- Roof leaks are one of the most common and potentially damaging types of leaks in homes, and can be caused by a variety of factors, such as aging or damaged shingles, improper flashing, or clogged gutters.
- Signs of a roof leak may include water stains or bubbling on ceilings or walls, dripping or running water during rain or snowmelt, or wet or sagging insulation in your attic.
- If left unchecked, roof leaks can lead to serious structural damage, mold growth, and other moisture-related issues, and can be costly to repair or replace.

  ii. Plumbing Leaks
- Plumbing leaks can occur in any part of your home's water supply or drainage system, and can be caused by factors such as corrosion, wear and tear, or improper installation or maintenance.

- Signs of a plumbing leak may include dripping or running water, wet or damp spots on floors or walls, low water pressure, or unexplained increases in your water bill.
- Plumbing leaks can cause significant water damage and waste, and can also create ideal conditions for mold and bacteria growth if not addressed promptly.

iii. Foundation Leaks

- Foundation leaks occur when water seeps through cracks, gaps, or other openings in your home's foundation walls or floor, and can be caused by factors such as poor drainage, hydrostatic pressure, or structural damage.
- Signs of a foundation leak may include water stains or efflorescence on basement walls or floors, musty odors or humid air, or cracks or shifting in your foundation or interior walls.
- Foundation leaks can lead to serious structural issues, as well as mold growth and other health hazards, and often require professional assessment and repair.

iv. Condensation and Humidity

- Condensation and humidity issues occur when excess moisture in the air condenses on cool surfaces, such as windows, pipes, or walls, and can be caused by factors such as poor ventilation, overcooling, or high indoor humidity levels.
- Signs of condensation and humidity issues may include foggy or frosty windows, damp or clammy walls or floors, musty odors, or visible mold or mildew growth.

- Condensation and humidity can lead to a range of moisture-related problems, such as wood rot, peeling paint, and allergies or respiratory issues, and often require a combination of ventilation, insulation, and humidity control measures to address.

b. Identifying and Diagnosing Leaks and Moisture Issues
i. Visual Inspection
- The first step in identifying leaks and moisture issues is to perform a thorough visual inspection of your home, both inside and out, looking for signs of water damage, staining, or other visible indicators.
- Pay particular attention to areas that are prone to moisture, such as bathrooms, kitchens, laundry rooms, basements, and attics, as well as areas around windows, doors, and plumbing fixtures.
- Use a flashlight, mirror, or other tools to check for hidden or hard-to-reach areas, such as behind appliances, under sinks, or in crawl spaces or utility closets.

ii. Moisture Meter Testing
- A moisture meter is a handheld device that can measure the moisture content of various building materials, such as wood, drywall, or concrete, and can help you identify areas of hidden or potential moisture damage.
- To use a moisture meter, simply press the probes or sensors against the surface you want to test, and read the moisture level on the display. Most meters will give you a percentage or relative humidity reading, with higher numbers indicating more moisture.

- Moisture meters can be particularly useful for detecting leaks or moisture issues behind walls, under flooring, or in other areas that may not show visible signs of damage, and can help you pinpoint the source and extent of the problem.

iii. Infrared Camera Imaging
- An infrared camera, also known as a thermal imaging camera, is a specialized tool that can detect temperature variations on surfaces, which can indicate the presence of moisture, air leaks, or other hidden issues.
- To use an infrared camera, simply point the camera at the area you want to inspect and look for any abnormal or unexpected temperature patterns, such as cool spots on a warm wall or hot spots on a cool surface.
- Infrared cameras can be particularly useful for identifying leaks or moisture issues in hard-to-reach or concealed areas, such as behind walls or under insulation, and can help you locate the source and path of the water or moisture.

iv. Professional Assessment
- If you suspect a serious or complex leak or moisture issue, or if you are unsure how to properly identify or diagnose the problem, it may be best to contact a professional home inspector, plumber, or waterproofing contractor for an assessment.
- A professional can use specialized tools and expertise to thoroughly evaluate your home's moisture and leak issues, identify the root causes and contributing factors, and recommend the most appropriate and effective solutions for your specific needs and budget.

- Professional assessments can also help you prioritize repairs and upgrades, and ensure that any work is done safely, effectively, and in compliance with local building codes and standards.

c. Fixing Leaks and Moisture Issues
i. Roof Repairs and Maintenance
- To fix roof leaks and prevent future moisture issues, you may need to repair or replace damaged or missing shingles, seal or flash around vents, chimneys, or other penetrations, or clean and maintain your gutters and downspouts.
- For minor repairs, such as replacing a few shingles or patching a small hole, you may be able to do the work yourself using a ladder, roofing nails, and roofing cement. However, for more extensive or complex repairs, it's best to hire a licensed roofing contractor to ensure proper installation and safety.
- To prevent future roof leaks and extend the life of your roof, it's important to perform regular inspections and maintenance, such as cleaning gutters, trimming overhanging branches, and replacing worn or damaged roofing materials as needed.

ii. Plumbing Repairs and Upgrades
- To fix plumbing leaks and prevent future moisture issues, you may need to repair or replace faulty or corroded pipes, fittings, or fixtures, or upgrade your plumbing system to meet current codes and standards.

- For minor repairs, such as replacing a washer or tightening a connection, you may be able to do the work yourself using basic plumbing tools and supplies. However, for more complex or extensive repairs, such as replacing a water heater or sewer line, it's best to hire a licensed plumber to ensure proper installation and safety.
- To prevent future plumbing leaks and improve your home's water efficiency, you may also want to consider upgrading to newer, more durable and efficient plumbing fixtures and appliances, such as low-flow toilets, water-saving showerheads, or tankless water heaters.

iii. Foundation Waterproofing and Drainage

- To fix foundation leaks and prevent future moisture issues, you may need to repair or seal cracks or gaps in your foundation walls or floor, install or improve your home's waterproofing and drainage systems, or address any underlying structural or soil issues.
- For minor cracks or gaps, you may be able to do the work yourself using hydraulic cement, masonry caulk, or other sealants. However, for more serious or extensive foundation issues, it's best to hire a licensed waterproofing or foundation repair contractor to ensure proper assessment and repair.
- To prevent future foundation leaks and moisture issues, it's important to ensure proper grading and drainage around your foundation, install and maintain gutters and downspouts, and address any sources of water or moisture near your foundation, such as irrigation systems, landscaping, or downspouts.

iv. Ventilation and Humidity Control
- To fix condensation and humidity issues and prevent future moisture problems, you may need to improve your home's ventilation and air circulation, control indoor humidity levels, or address any sources of excess moisture, such as cooking, bathing, or laundry.
- For minor ventilation issues, you may be able to do the work yourself by installing exhaust fans, opening windows, or using dehumidifiers or air purifiers. However, for more complex or whole-house ventilation needs, it's best to consult with a licensed HVAC contractor or indoor air quality specialist.
- To prevent future condensation and humidity issues, it's important to maintain proper indoor humidity levels (ideally between 30-50%), use exhaust fans in bathrooms and kitchens, seal air leaks and improve insulation, and address any sources of excess moisture or water vapor in your home.

d. Preventing Future Leaks and Moisture Issues
i. Regular Inspections and Maintenance
- One of the best ways to prevent leaks and moisture issues is to perform regular inspections and maintenance on your home's roof, plumbing, foundation, and ventilation systems.
- This may include cleaning gutters and downspouts, checking for leaks or damage, replacing worn or damaged materials, and ensuring proper function and efficiency of all systems and components.

- By catching and addressing small issues early, you can often prevent them from turning into larger, more costly problems down the road, and can extend the life and value of your home.

ii. Proper Landscaping and Drainage
- Another key factor in preventing leaks and moisture issues is to ensure proper landscaping and drainage around your home's foundation and exterior.
- This may include grading the soil to slope away from your foundation, installing and maintaining gutters and downspouts, avoiding overwatering or directing water towards your foundation, and choosing moisture-tolerant landscaping plants and materials.
- By keeping water and moisture away from your home's structure and foundation, you can reduce the risk of leaks, damage, and other moisture-related issues.

iii. Upgrading and Retrofitting
- In some cases, preventing future leaks and moisture issues may require upgrading or retrofitting your home's systems and components to meet current codes, standards, and best practices.
- This may include installing new roofing, plumbing, or waterproofing materials, adding insulation or air sealing, or upgrading your ventilation or humidity control systems.
- While these upgrades can be costly upfront, they can often pay for themselves over time through increased energy efficiency, reduced maintenance and repair costs, and improved home value and comfort.

iv. Educating and Empowering Homeowners
- Finally, one of the most important ways to prevent leaks and moisture issues is to educate and empower homeowners to take an active role in maintaining and protecting their homes.
- This may include providing resources and guidance on home maintenance and repair, offering incentives or financing for home upgrades and retrofits, and promoting awareness and understanding of the importance of moisture control and indoor air quality.
- By working together as a community to prioritize and address these issues, we can create healthier, more sustainable, and more resilient homes and neighborhoods for generations to come.

In conclusion, identifying and fixing leaks and moisture issues is a critical aspect of home maintenance and protection, and requires a combination of knowledge, skills, and resources. By understanding the common types and signs of leaks and moisture problems, using the right tools and techniques to diagnose and assess them, and taking prompt and appropriate action to repair and prevent them, homeowners can safeguard the health, safety, and value of their homes, and enjoy a more comfortable and worry-free living experience. Whether you are a new homeowner or a seasoned pro, investing in leak and moisture control is one of the best things you can do for your home and your family.

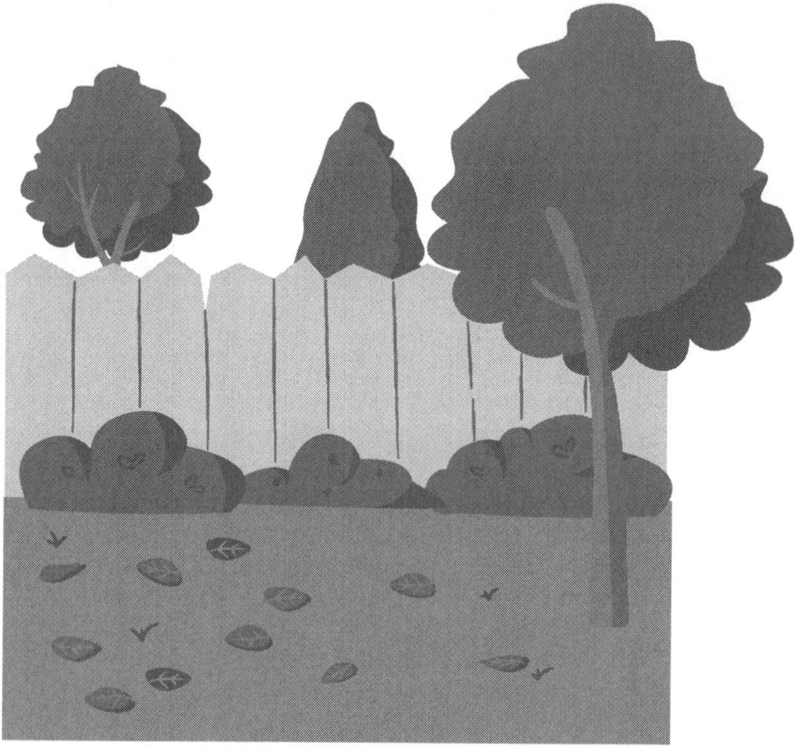

Chapter 5
DIY Drainage Projects and Maintenance
Tools and Materials for Yard Drainage Projects

When tackling DIY drainage projects in your yard, having the right tools and materials is essential for ensuring a successful outcome. From basic hand tools to specialized equipment, the tools and materials you'll need will depend on the scope and complexity of your project, as well as your own skills and experience level. In this section, we'll explore some of the most common and essential tools and materials for yard drainage projects, and provide tips and guidance on how to choose and use them effectively.

a. Basic Hand Tools
   i. Shovels and Spades
- Shovels and spades are the most basic and essential tools for any yard drainage project, and are used for digging, excavating, and moving soil and other materials.
- There are many different types and sizes of shovels and spades, each designed for specific tasks and soil conditions. For example, a pointed spade is best for cutting through roots and tough soil, while a flat spade is better for scooping and lifting loose soil.
- When choosing a shovel or spade, look for one with a sturdy, comfortable handle and a sharp, durable blade that is appropriate for your soil type and project needs.

ii. Rakes and Hoes
- Rakes and hoes are used for grading, leveling, and smoothing soil surfaces, as well as for removing rocks, roots, and other debris from your work area.
- There are several types of rakes and hoes, including garden rakes, bow rakes, and grading hoes, each with different tine or blade configurations and purposes.
- When choosing a rake or hoe, look for one with a strong, lightweight handle and a head that is appropriate for your soil type and project needs.

iii. Hammers and Mallets
- Hammers and mallets are used for driving stakes, posts, and other supports into the ground, as well as for shaping and fitting drainage materials like pipes and fittings.
- There are many types of hammers and mallets, including claw hammers, rubber mallets, and dead blow hammers, each with different weights, materials, and striking surfaces.
- When choosing a hammer or mallet, look for one with a comfortable grip and a head that is appropriate for your project needs and materials.

iv. Levels and Measuring Tools
- Levels and measuring tools are used for ensuring proper slope, alignment, and depth of your drainage features, as well as for marking and cutting materials to size.
- There are many types of levels and measuring tools, including bubble levels, laser levels, tape measures, and marking paint or flags.
- When choosing levels and measuring tools, look for ones that are accurate, durable, and easy to read and use in outdoor conditions.

b. Power Tools and Equipment

i. Drills and Augers

- Drills and augers are used for boring holes in soil, rock, or other materials, as well as for driving screws, bolts, and other fasteners.
- There are many types of drills and augers, including hand-held drills, post hole diggers, and power augers, each with different sizes, speeds, and power sources.
- When choosing a drill or auger, look for one with a powerful motor, adjustable speed and torque settings, and a chuck or bit that is compatible with your project needs and materials.

ii. Saws and Cutters

- Saws and cutters are used for cutting and shaping drainage pipes, boards, and other materials to size and fit.
- There are many types of saws and cutters, including hacksaws, reciprocating saws, and pipe cutters, each with different blade types, sizes, and cutting capacities.
- When choosing a saw or cutter, look for one with a sharp, durable blade that is appropriate for your material type and thickness, as well as a comfortable grip and safety features like guards or locks.

iii. Compactors and Tampers

- Compactors and tampers are used for compressing and stabilizing soil, gravel, and other fill materials, as well as for leveling and smoothing surfaces.
- There are several types of compactors and tampers, including plate compactors, jumping jacks, and hand tampers, each with different sizes, weights, and compaction forces.

- When choosing a compactor or tamper, look for one with a powerful engine or impact force, adjustable speed and depth settings, and a base plate or foot that is appropriate for your soil type and project needs.

iv. Trenchers and Excavators
- Trenchers and excavators are used for digging and shaping trenches, channels, and other drainage features, as well as for removing and hauling soil and debris.
- There are many types of trenchers and excavators, including walk-behind trenchers, mini excavators, and backhoes, each with different sizes, depths, and bucket or blade configurations.
- When choosing a trencher or excavator, look for one with a powerful engine or hydraulic system, adjustable depth and width settings, and a boom, arm, or chain that is appropriate for your soil type and project scope.

c. **Drainage Materials and Supplies**
i. Pipes and Fittings
- Pipes and fittings are the backbone of most yard drainage systems, and are used for collecting, conveying, and discharging water from your property.
- There are many types of drainage pipes and fittings, including PVC, ABS, corrugated plastic, and metal, each with different sizes, lengths, and connection types.
- When choosing pipes and fittings, look for ones that are durable, corrosion-resistant, and rated for your specific application and burial depth, as well as compatible with your other drainage components and local building codes.

ii. Catch Basins and Grates
- Catch basins and grates are used for collecting and filtering water from surface runoff, as well as for providing access to underground drainage pipes and systems.
- There are several types of catch basins and grates, including pre-cast concrete, plastic, and metal, each with different sizes, shapes, and load ratings.
- When choosing catch basins and grates, look for ones that are sturdy, non-clogging, and appropriate for your expected water flow and debris load, as well as compatible with your pipes and other drainage components.

iii. Gravel and Aggregates
- Gravel and aggregates are used for filling and stabilizing drainage trenches, as well as for improving soil drainage and preventing erosion around pipes and other features.
- There are many types of gravel and aggregates, including washed gravel, crushed stone, and pea gravel, each with different sizes, colors, and drainage properties.
- When choosing gravel and aggregates, look for ones that are clean, uniform, and appropriate for your soil type and drainage needs, as well as compatible with your pipes and other system components.

iv. Geotextiles and Membranes
- Geotextiles and membranes are used for lining and filtering drainage trenches, as well as for separating soil layers and preventing soil migration and clogging.
- There are many types of geotextiles and membranes, including woven and non-woven fabrics, perforated and solid plastics, and biodegradable and permanent materials.

- When choosing geotextiles and membranes, look for ones that are permeable, durable, and appropriate for your soil type and drainage application, as well as compatible with your pipes, aggregates, and other system components.

d. Safety and Maintenance Equipment
i. Gloves and Eye Protection
- Gloves and eye protection are essential for preventing cuts, scrapes, and other injuries when working with tools, materials, and debris.
- Look for gloves that are sturdy, flexible, and appropriate for your hand size and project needs, as well as eye protection that is impact-resistant, fog-free, and comfortable to wear for extended periods.

ii. Boots and Clothing
- Proper footwear and clothing are important for preventing slips, trips, and other accidents when working in wet, muddy, or uneven conditions.
- Look for boots that are waterproof, slip-resistant, and supportive, as well as clothing that is durable, breathable, and appropriate for the weather and working conditions.

iii. First Aid and Emergency Supplies
- Having basic first aid and emergency supplies on hand is important for treating minor injuries and responding to unexpected situations that may arise during your project.
- Keep a well-stocked first-aid kit, as well as a charged phone, flashlight, and other emergency essentials, in a easily accessible location on your project site.

iv. Maintenance and Repair Tools
- Regular maintenance and repair of your drainage system is important for ensuring its long-term performance and effectiveness.
- Keep a set of basic maintenance and repair tools, such as a drain snake, pipe wrench, and sealant, as well as spare parts like gaskets and fittings, on hand for quick fixes and preventive maintenance tasks.

By having the right tools and materials for your yard drainage project, you can work more efficiently, effectively, and safely, and achieve better results with less frustration and wasted effort. Whether you are a seasoned DIYer or a first-time landscaper, investing in quality tools and materials is one of the best ways to ensure a successful and rewarding project outcome.

Step-by-Step Guides for Common Drainage Installations

Installing proper drainage systems in your yard is essential for preventing water damage, erosion, and other landscaping issues. While every yard is unique and may require customized solutions, there are several common drainage installations that can be tackled by DIYers with the right tools, materials, and guidance. In this section, we'll provide step-by-step guides for some of the most common and effective yard drainage installations, including French drains, dry wells, and swales.

a. French Drain Installation
   i. Planning and Preparation
- Determine the location and length of your French drain based on your yard's topography, soil type, and water flow patterns.
- Mark the planned path of your drain with stakes, string, or spray paint, and call your local utility companies to locate any underground lines or pipes before digging.
- Gather your tools and materials, including a trenching shovel, level, perforated pipe, gravel, landscape fabric, and end cap or outlet.

   ii. Excavation and Grading
- Dig a trench along your planned path, typically 6-12 inches wide and 18-24 inches deep, depending on your soil type and water flow volume.
- Grade the bottom of the trench to slope towards your desired outlet point, using a level and string to ensure a consistent 1-2% grade.

- Remove any roots, rocks, or debris from the trench, and smooth the bottom and sides to prevent damage to your pipe or fabric.

iii. Pipe and Gravel Installation
- Line the bottom and sides of the trench with permeable landscape fabric, overlapping the edges by at least 6 inches to prevent soil migration.
- Place a 2-3 inch layer of clean, washed gravel (1/2 to 3/4 inch size) on top of the fabric, and smooth it to create a level bed for your pipe.
- Lay your perforated pipe on top of the gravel bed, with the perforations facing down, and connect any fittings or end caps as needed.
- Cover the pipe with another 2-3 inch layer of gravel, filling the trench to within 6 inches of the surface.

iv. Backfilling and Finishing
- Wrap the excess landscape fabric over the top of the gravel layer, overlapping the edges to create a barrier against soil intrusion
- Backfill the remaining trench with native soil, tamping it gently to remove air pockets and create a slightly mounded surface to allow for settling.
- Finish the surface with sod, seed, or other landscaping materials as desired, and water thoroughly to settle the soil and establish vegetation.

b. Dry Well Installation

i. Planning and Preparation
- Determine the location and size of your dry well based on your yard's water flow patterns, soil type, and available space.

- Mark the planned location of your dry well with stakes or spray paint, and call your local utility companies to locate any underground lines or pipes before digging.
- Gather your tools and materials, including a post hole digger or excavator, level, perforated barrel or chamber, gravel, landscape fabric, and lid or cover.

ii. Excavation and Leveling
- Dig a hole at your planned location, typically 3-5 feet wide and 3-5 feet deep, depending on your soil type and expected water volume.
- Level the bottom of the hole and remove any roots, rocks, or debris to create a stable base for your dry well.
- If your soil is poorly draining or contains a lot of clay, you may need to over-excavate the hole and backfill with gravel or sand to improve drainage.

iii. Barrel or Chamber Installation
- Line the bottom and sides of the hole with permeable landscape fabric, overlapping the edges by at least 6 inches to prevent soil migration.
- Place a 2-3 inch layer of clean, washed gravel (1/2 to 3/4 inch size) on top of the fabric, and smooth it to create a level bed for your barrel or chamber.
- Place your perforated barrel or chamber on top of the gravel bed, making sure it is level and stable.
- If using a barrel, drill additional holes in the sides and bottom to increase drainage capacity, and wrap the entire barrel in landscape fabric to prevent soil intrusion.

iv. Backfilling and Finishing
- Fill the space around the barrel or chamber with clean, washed gravel, up to the top of the barrel or within 6 inches of the surface.

- Wrap the excess landscape fabric over the top of the gravel layer, overlapping the edges to create a barrier against soil intrusion.
- Backfill the remaining hole with native soil, tamping it gently to remove air pockets and create a slightly mounded surface to allow for settling.
- Install a sturdy lid or cover over the top of the dry well to prevent debris and animals from entering, and to provide a safe and attractive finish.

c. Swale Installation

i. Planning and Preparation
- Determine the location and dimensions of your swale based on your yard's topography, soil type, and water flow patterns.
- Mark the planned path of your swale with stakes, string, or spray paint, and consider any existing landscaping or structures that may need to be avoided or modified.
- Gather your tools and materials, including a sod cutter or spade, level, rake, compost or topsoil, and grass seed or sod.

ii. Excavation and Grading
- Remove any existing grass, vegetation, or debris from the path of your swale using a sod cutter or spade.
- Dig a shallow, broad trench along your planned path, typically 6-12 inches deep and 2-4 feet wide, depending on your soil type and expected water volume.
- Grade the bottom of the trench to slope towards your desired outlet point, using a level and string to ensure a consistent 1-2% grade.

- Create gently sloping sides on either side of the trench, with a maximum slope of 3:1 (horizontal to vertical) to prevent erosion and allow for easy mowing.

iii. Soil Amendment and Smoothing
- If your soil is compacted or poorly draining, loosen it with a garden fork or rototiller to a depth of 6-8 inches to improve infiltration.
- Mix in a 2-3 inch layer of compost, topsoil, or other organic matter to improve soil structure and fertility, and to provide a better growing medium for grass or other vegetation.
- Rake the amended soil smooth and level, removing any rocks, roots, or debris, and creating a slight concave shape to the bottom of the swale.

iv. Seeding and Finishing
- Spread a generous amount of grass seed over the entire swale area, using a mix that is appropriate for your climate, soil type, and sunlight conditions.
- Rake the seed lightly into the soil to ensure good seed-to-soil contact, and cover with a thin layer of straw or other mulch to retain moisture and prevent erosion.
- Water the seeded area thoroughly and regularly until the grass is well established, typically 2-3 times per day for the first 2-3 weeks, depending on weather conditions.
- Alternatively, you can lay sod over the swale area for a quicker and more polished finish, making sure to stagger the seams and water thoroughly to encourage root growth.

By following these step-by-step guides for common drainage installations, you can create effective and attractive solutions for managing water flow and preventing damage in your yard. Whether you choose a French drain, dry well, swale, or a combination of techniques, be sure to plan carefully, work safely, and maintain your drainage systems regularly to ensure optimal performance and longevity. With a little knowledge, effort, and patience, you can transform your yard into a beautiful and functional landscape that manages water wisely and sustainably.

Maintenance Checklist for Drainage Systems

Regular maintenance is essential for ensuring the long-term performance and effectiveness of your yard drainage systems. By following a consistent maintenance schedule and checklist, you can prevent clogs, leaks, and other issues that can compromise your drainage and lead to costly repairs or damage. In this section, we'll provide a detailed maintenance checklist for common yard drainage systems, including gutters and downspouts, French drains, dry wells, and swales.

a. Gutters and Downspouts
  i. Cleaning and Inspection (Every 3-6 months)
Remove any debris, such as leaves, twigs, and shingle grit, from your gutters and downspouts using a ladder, gloves, and a garden trowel or gutter scoop.
- Flush your gutters and downspouts with a hose to remove any remaining debris and check for proper water flow and drainage.
- Inspect your gutters and downspouts for any signs of damage, such as cracks, holes, rust, or sagging, and repair or replace as needed.
- Check the gutter hangers and downspout fasteners for tightness and stability, and adjust or replace as needed to ensure proper alignment and support.

  ii. Repairs and Upgrades (As needed)
- Seal any leaks or holes in your gutters or downspouts using a compatible sealant or patch kit, following the manufacturer's instructions for application and curing.

- Replace any severely damaged or corroded sections of gutter or downspout with new materials that match the existing system in size, shape, and color.
- Consider upgrading your gutters with gutter guards, screens, or covers to prevent debris buildup and reduce maintenance needs.
- Install or repair splash blocks, extensions, or underground drainage pipes to ensure that water is directed away from your foundation and into appropriate drainage areas.

b. French Drains

i. Cleaning and Inspection (Every 6-12 months)
- Check the outlet or discharge point of your French drain to ensure that it is clear of debris, erosion, or other obstructions that could impede water flow.
- Remove any accumulated sediment, leaves, or other debris from the outlet using a shovel, rake, or hose.
- Walk the length of your French drain, looking for any signs of settling, clogging, or damage to the surface or vegetation, such as sinkholes, wet spots, or dead grass.
- If you notice any issues, carefully excavate a small section of the drain to check for pipe damage, gravel clogging, or fabric tears, and repair or replace as needed.

ii. Repairs and Upgrades (As needed)
- If your French drain is clogged or damaged, excavate the affected section and remove the gravel, fabric, and pipe for cleaning or replacement.
- Flush the pipe with a hose or pressure washer to remove any sediment or roots, and check for holes, cracks, or other damage that may require repair or replacement.

- Replace any damaged or clogged fabric or gravel with new materials that match the existing system in type, size, and permeability.
- Consider upgrading your French drain with a larger diameter pipe, additional cleanouts or inspection ports, or a more durable fabric or gravel layer to improve performance and longevity.

c. Dry Wells
i. Cleaning and Inspection (Every 6-12 months)
- Check the inlet and outlet of your dry well to ensure that they are clear of debris, sediment, or other obstructions that could impede water flow.
- Remove any accumulated debris or sediment from the inlet and outlet using a shovel, rake, or hose.
- Inspect the lid or cover of your dry well for any signs of damage, such as cracks, rust, or loose fasteners, and repair or replace as needed to ensure a secure and safe fit.
- If you notice any signs of settling, ponding, or overflow around your dry well, carefully excavate a small section to check for gravel clogging, fabric tears, or barrel damage, and repair or replace as needed.

ii. Repairs and Upgrades (As needed)
- If your dry well is clogged or damaged, excavate the affected area and remove the gravel, fabric, and barrel for cleaning or replacement.
- Inspect the barrel for any holes, cracks, or other damage that may require repair or replacement, and clean or flush the barrel with a hose or pressure washer to remove any sediment or debris.

- Replace any damaged or clogged fabric or gravel with new materials that match the existing system in type, size, and permeability.
- Consider upgrading your dry well with a larger barrel or chamber, additional perforations or drainage holes, or a more durable fabric or gravel layer to improve infiltration and storage capacity.

d. Swales
i. Inspection and Mowing (Every 1-3 months)
- Walk the length of your swale, looking for any signs of erosion, sediment buildup, or damage to the grass or vegetation, such as bare spots, rills, or gullies.
- Check the inlet and outlet of your swale to ensure that they are clear of debris, rocks, or other obstructions that could impede water flow or cause flooding.
- Mow the grass in your swale to a height of 2-4 inches, using a mulching mower or grass catcher to prevent clippings from clogging the swale or outlet.
- Trim any overhanging branches, shrubs, or other vegetation that could obstruct water flow or drop debris into the swale.

ii. Repairs and Improvements (As needed)
- If you notice any eroded or bare areas in your swale, fill them with topsoil or compost and reseed or sod the area to establish new grass growth and prevent further erosion.
- If your swale has significant sediment buildup or blockages, use a shovel or rake to remove the excess material and restore the original shape and grade of the swale.

- If your swale is not draining properly or has standing water, consider regrading the swale to increase the slope, improve the soil drainage, or install an underdrain or overflow outlet to prevent ponding and mosquito breeding.
- Consider enhancing your swale with native plants, rock borders, or other landscaping features to improve its appearance, biodiversity, and water quality benefits, while still maintaining its drainage function.

By following this comprehensive maintenance checklist for your yard drainage systems, you can ensure optimal performance, prevent problems, and extend the life of your investment. Whether you have gutters, French drains, dry wells, swales, or a combination of systems, regular cleaning, inspection, and repairs are key to maintaining effective and efficient drainage in your yard. By staying proactive and vigilant, you can avoid costly damage, protect your property value, and enjoy a beautiful and functional landscape for years to come.

Troubleshooting Common Drainage Problems

Even with proper design, installation, and maintenance, yard drainage systems can sometimes experience problems that affect their performance and functionality. From clogs and leaks to erosion and ponding, these issues can lead to water damage, landscape deterioration, and other headaches for homeowners. In this section, we'll explore some of the most common drainage problems and provide troubleshooting tips and solutions to help you identify and resolve them quickly and effectively.

a. Clogged Gutters and Downspouts
  i. Symptoms
- Water overflowing or spilling from gutters during rain events
- Sagging or pulling away of gutters from roof or fascia
- Visible accumulation of debris, such as leaves, twigs, or shingle grit, in gutters or downspouts
- Water stains or damage on siding, foundation, or landscaping below gutters

  ii. Causes
- Lack of regular cleaning and maintenance
- Nearby trees or vegetation shedding leaves, needles, or seeds into gutters
- Deterioration or damage to gutter or downspout materials, such as rust, cracks, or holes
- Improper installation or slope of gutters or downspouts

iii. Solutions
- Clean gutters and downspouts thoroughly using a ladder, gloves, and a garden trowel or gutter scoop, removing all debris and flushing with a hose to check for proper drainage.
- Trim nearby trees or vegetation to reduce the amount of debris falling into gutters, or consider installing gutter guards or covers to prevent clogs.
- Repair or seal any leaks, holes, or damage to gutters or downspouts using a compatible sealant or patch kit, or replace severely deteriorated sections with new materials.
- Adjust the slope of gutters or downspouts to ensure proper drainage, aiming for a minimum slope of 1/4 inch per foot of run, and reattach any loose or sagging sections with new hangers or fasteners.

b. French Drain Failure

i. Symptoms
- Water pooling or ponding in areas near the French drain
- Wet or soggy spots in the lawn or landscaping above the French drain
- Slow or no drainage from the French drain outlet or discharge point
- Sinkhole or settlement of soil above the French drain

ii. Causes
- Clogging of the perforated pipe or gravel layer with sediment, roots, or other debris
- Collapse or breakage of the perforated pipe due to improper installation, soil settlement, or heavy loads

- Damage or clogging of the drainage fabric or filter layer, allowing soil to mix with the gravel and impede water flow
- Insufficient slope or capacity of the French drain system to handle the water volume or flow rate

iii. Solutions
- Locate and excavate the affected section of the French drain, removing the gravel, fabric, and pipe for inspection and cleaning.
- Flush the perforated pipe with a hose or pressure washer to remove any clogs or debris, and check for any cracks, holes, or other damage that may require repair or replacement.
- Replace any damaged or clogged drainage fabric or gravel with new materials that match the original specifications, ensuring proper overlap and coverage to prevent soil intrusion.
- Regrade or deepen the French drain trench as needed to increase the slope or capacity of the system, and consider adding additional cleanouts, inspection ports, or outlet points to improve maintenance access and drainage performance.

c. Dry Well Overflow

i. Symptoms
- Water ponding or flooding around the dry well during heavy rain events
- Slow or no drainage of water into the dry well inlet or barrel
- Wet or mushy soil around the perimeter of the dry well
- Unpleasant odors or mosquito breeding in the dry well area

ii. Causes
- Overloading of the dry well with too much water or debris, exceeding its storage or infiltration capacity
- Clogging of the barrel, gravel, or fabric layer with sediment, roots, or other debris, preventing water from entering or exiting the dry well
- Compaction or saturation of the surrounding soil, reducing its ability to absorb and percolate water away from the dry well
- Improper sizing, design, or location of the dry well system for the specific soil, water, and site conditions

iii. Solutions
- Reduce the amount of water entering the dry well by redirecting roof runoff, sump pump discharge, or other sources to alternate drainage areas or systems.
- Excavate and clean out the dry well barrel, removing any accumulated sediment, debris, or roots, and flushing the barrel and gravel layer with a hose or pressure washer to restore porosity and drainage.
- Replace any damaged or clogged fabric, gravel, or barrel components with new materials that meet the original design specifications, and consider increasing the size or depth of the dry well to improve storage and infiltration capacity.
- Improve the drainage and permeability of the surrounding soil by amending with sand, compost, or other organic matter, and consider installing additional overflow drains, swales, or other backup drainage systems to handle excess water during peak flows.

d. Swale Erosion and Sedimentation

i. Symptoms
- Formation of rills, gullies, or bare spots in the swale channel or side slopes
- Accumulation of sediment, debris, or vegetation at the swale outlet or along the swale bottom
- Ponding or stagnation of water in the swale, especially after rain events
- Widening or deepening of the swale channel over time, or loss of original shape and grade

ii. Causes
- Excessive water velocity or volume in the swale, exceeding the erosion resistance of the soil or vegetation
- Lack of proper stabilization or reinforcement of the swale surface, such as grass, mulch, or erosion control blankets
- Steep or uneven side slopes that promote soil slumping, sliding, or collapse into the swale channel
- Poor soil quality or fertility that inhibits healthy vegetation growth and root development for erosion control

iii. Solutions
- Regrade or reshape the swale channel and side slopes as needed to restore the original design dimensions, slope, and cross-section, using a level and excavation tools to ensure proper alignment and drainage.
- Install erosion control measures such as sod, seed, mulch, or erosion control blankets to stabilize the swale surface and prevent further soil loss, following the manufacturer's instructions for application and maintenance.

- Consider adding check dams, rock weirs, or other flow control structures along the swale channel to reduce water velocity, promote infiltration, and trap sediment before it reaches the outlet.
- Amend the swale soil with compost, topsoil, or other organic matter to improve fertility, structure, and water-holding capacity, and choose grass or plant species that are well-suited to the specific soil, moisture, and sunlight conditions of the site.

By understanding these common drainage problems and their symptoms, causes, and solutions, you can better diagnose and address any issues that may arise in your own yard drainage systems. Whether you need to clean your gutters, repair your French drain, upgrade your dry well, or restore your swale, following these troubleshooting tips and best practices can help you keep your drainage systems functioning properly and effectively for years to come. Of course, if you encounter a problem that is beyond your skill level or comfort zone, don't hesitate to contact a professional landscaper, drainage contractor, or engineer for expert advice and assistance.

Chapter 6
When to Hire a Professional
Signs You Need Professional Help

While many yard drainage problems can be prevented or resolved through proper design, installation, and maintenance, there are some situations where hiring a professional is the best course of action. Whether you're dealing with complex site conditions, severe water damage, or outdated or failing drainage systems, a qualified and experienced professional can provide the expertise, tools, and resources needed to diagnose and address the issue effectively and efficiently. In this section, we'll explore some of the key signs that indicate you may need professional help with your yard drainage, and provide guidance on when and how to seek out the right expertise for your specific needs and budget.

a. Complex or Challenging Site Conditions
  i. Steep Slopes or Uneven Terrain
- If your yard has steep slopes, hills, or uneven terrain that makes it difficult to control water flow or install traditional drainage systems, a professional can help you design and implement a customized solution that works with your specific site conditions.
- A professional can use specialized tools and techniques, such as terracing, retaining walls, or subsurface drainage systems, to manage water flow and prevent erosion on steep or challenging sites.

ii. Poor Soil Quality or Hydrology
- If your yard has heavy clay, compacted, or poorly draining soils that prevent water from infiltrating or percolating properly, a professional can help you identify the underlying soil characteristics and recommend appropriate drainage solutions.
- A professional can use soil testing, percolation tests, or other diagnostic tools to determine the soil texture, structure, and hydraulic conductivity, and design a drainage system that is tailored to your specific soil conditions.

iii. High Water Table or Groundwater Issues
- If your yard has a high water table or is prone to groundwater seepage, springs, or other subsurface water issues, a professional can help you identify the source and extent of the problem and recommend appropriate mitigation strategies.
- A professional can use monitoring wells, piezometers, or other hydrogeologic tools to measure and map the water table and groundwater flow patterns, and design a drainage system that intercepts, collects, and redirects the excess water away from your home and landscape.

b. Severe Water Damage or Property Impacts
 i. Foundation or Structural Damage
- If you notice cracks, settling, or other signs of structural damage to your home's foundation, walls, or other load-bearing elements, it may be a sign of severe water infiltration or drainage problems that require professional assessment and repair.

- A professional can use specialized diagnostic tools, such as moisture meters, infrared cameras, or soil borings, to identify the source and extent of the water damage, and recommend appropriate waterproofing, drainage, or structural repairs to prevent further deterioration.

ii. Persistent Flooding or Ponding
- If your yard experiences frequent or persistent flooding, ponding, or water accumulation, even after heavy rain events have ended, it may be a sign of inadequate or failing drainage systems that require professional evaluation and upgrades.
- A professional can use hydrologic modeling, site surveys, or other analytical tools to identify the drainage patterns, capacities, and limitations of your current systems, and recommend appropriate modifications, replacements, or additions to improve drainage performance and prevent future flooding.

iii. Significant Erosion or Soil Loss
- If you observe significant erosion, gullying, or soil loss in your yard, especially on slopes, hillsides, or along drainage channels, it may be a sign of excessive water flow, velocity, or volume that requires professional stabilization and control measures.
- A professional can use erosion control blankets, geotextiles, vegetation, or other best management practices to stabilize and protect the soil surface, and design drainage systems that reduce the erosive power of water and promote infiltration and sediment trapping.

c. Outdated or Failing Drainage Infrastructure

i. Aging or Deteriorating Components
- If your yard drainage systems are old, deteriorated, or no longer functioning as designed, it may be time to hire a professional to assess their condition and recommend appropriate repairs, replacements, or upgrades.
- A professional can use video inspection, pressure testing, or other diagnostic tools to identify the location, extent, and cause of any leaks, clogs, or other failures in your drainage pipes, culverts, or other components, and recommend cost-effective and durable solutions.

ii. Non-Compliant or Illegal Systems
- If your yard drainage systems were installed before current codes, regulations, or best practices were in place, or if they were installed without proper permits, approvals, or inspections, they may be non-compliant or illegal and require professional correction or replacement.
- A professional can help you navigate the complex web of local, state, and federal laws, standards, and requirements for yard drainage systems, and ensure that any new or retrofitted systems are designed, installed, and maintained in accordance with applicable regulations and best practices.

iii. Lack of Maintenance or Performance Records
- If you have no records or documentation of when your yard drainage systems were installed, maintained, or repaired, or if you have observed a gradual or sudden decline in their performance or effectiveness, it may be time to hire a professional to assess their condition and recommend appropriate actions.

- A professional can use their expertise and experience to identify the age, materials, and design of your existing drainage systems, and provide guidance on the expected lifespan, maintenance needs, and performance standards for each component, as well as recommendations for optimization or replacement if needed.

d. Limited Time, Skills, or Resources for DIY
i. Lack of Knowledge or Experience
- If you have limited knowledge or experience with yard drainage principles, practices, or technologies, attempting a DIY installation or repair may result in costly mistakes, delays, or even safety hazards.
- A professional has the education, training, and expertise to diagnose drainage problems accurately, select appropriate solutions, and implement them safely and effectively, using industry-standard tools, techniques, and quality control measures.

ii. Insufficient Tools or Equipment
- If you don't have access to the specialized tools, equipment, or materials needed for a particular drainage project, such as excavators, trenchers, or trenchless technologies, it may be more cost-effective and efficient to hire a professional who already has these resources and knows how to use them properly.
- A professional can leverage their existing inventory, supplier relationships, and economies of scale to provide the necessary tools, equipment, and materials for your project, often at a lower cost or higher quality than what you could obtain on your own.

iii. Time Constraints or Competing Priorities
- If you have a busy schedule, competing priorities, or a tight timeline for completing a yard drainage project, hiring a professional may be the best way to ensure that the work is done quickly, efficiently, and to a high standard of quality.
- A professional can dedicate their full attention, effort, and expertise to your project, without the distractions, interruptions, or learning curves that often come with DIY projects, and can often complete the work faster and with fewer delays or mishaps than a novice or part-time installer.

By recognizing these signs and situations where professional help may be needed for your yard drainage problems, you can make an informed and proactive decision about when and how to seek out the right expertise and support. Whether you need a one-time consultation, a full-scale installation, or ongoing maintenance and monitoring services, a qualified and reputable drainage professional can provide the knowledge, skills, and resources to help you achieve your goals and protect your property value and quality of life. Of course, the specific scope, cost, and timeline of professional services will vary depending on your unique site conditions, drainage needs, and budget, so it's important to do your research, ask for references, and get multiple bids before hiring any contractor or consultant.

Choosing the Right Contractor for Your Drainage Project

Once you've determined that you need professional help with your yard drainage project, the next critical step is to choose the right contractor for the job. With so many options and variables to consider, from qualifications and experience to cost and availability, selecting the best contractor can feel like a daunting task. However, by following some key criteria and best practices, you can narrow down your choices, evaluate your options, and ultimately hire a contractor who meets your specific needs, budget, and expectations. In this section, we'll provide a detailed guide on how to choose the right contractor for your yard drainage project, including what to look for, what to ask, and what to expect throughout the process.

a. Qualifications and Credentials
   i. Licensing and Insurance
- One of the first things to look for when choosing a drainage contractor is proper licensing and insurance. Depending on your state or local regulations, contractors may be required to hold specific licenses, certifications, or registrations to perform drainage work legally and safely.
- Ask potential contractors for proof of their licensing status, as well as their insurance coverage, including general liability, workers' compensation, and any other applicable policies. Verify the validity and expiration dates of these documents, and ensure that the coverage limits are adequate for your project scope and risk level.

ii. Professional Affiliations and Certifications
- Another important qualifier for drainage contractors is their professional affiliations and certifications. Membership in industry organizations, such as the National Association of Landscape Professionals (NALP) or the Interlocking Concrete Pavement Institute (ICPI), can demonstrate a contractor's commitment to professionalism, education, and best practices.
- Look for contractors who have earned relevant certifications, such as the Certified Landscape Irrigation Auditor (CLIA) or the Certified Erosion, Sediment, and Stormwater Inspector (CESSWI), which signify their specialized knowledge and skills in drainage-related fields.

iii. Education and Training
- Beyond formal credentials, it's also valuable to consider a contractor's education and training background. Ask about their academic degrees, technical training, or continuing education courses related to drainage design, installation, or maintenance.
- Look for contractors who invest in ongoing learning and development, such as attending industry conferences, workshops, or webinars, to stay current with the latest technologies, regulations, and best practices in the field.

b. Experience and Reputation

i. Years in Business and Project Portfolio
- When evaluating drainage contractors, consider their years of experience and the breadth and depth of their project portfolio. Look for contractors who have been in business for several years and have a proven track

- record of successfully completing projects similar in scope, scale, and complexity to yours.
- Ask for examples of their previous work, including photos, case studies, or references from past clients. Pay attention to the quality, creativity, and functionality of their designs, as well as their ability to meet deadlines, budgets, and customer expectations.

ii. Customer References and Reviews

- One of the best ways to gauge a contractor's reputation and customer satisfaction is to ask for references from their previous clients. Contact these references directly and ask about their experience working with the contractor, including their communication, professionalism, and quality of work.
- Look for patterns or trends in the feedback, such as consistent praise or criticism for certain aspects of the contractor's performance. Also, consider the relevance and recency of the references, giving more weight to projects that are similar to yours and have been completed within the past few years.

iii. Online Presence and Reputation

- In addition to personal references, research the contractor's online presence and reputation through their website, social media profiles, and third-party review sites like Yelp, Angie's List, or HomeAdvisor.
- Look for signs of professionalism, transparency, and customer engagement, such as clear and informative website content, prompt and courteous responses to customer inquiries or complaints, and a consistent brand identity and messaging across all platforms.

c. Service Offerings and Capabilities

i. Scope of Services and Specialization

- When choosing a drainage contractor, consider the scope of services they offer and their areas of specialization. Some contractors may provide a full range of drainage services, from design and installation to maintenance and repair, while others may focus on specific niches or technologies, such as french drains, permeable pavers, or rainwater harvesting.
- Look for contractors whose service offerings align with your project needs and goals, and who have demonstrated expertise and experience in the specific drainage solutions you're seeking. Ask about their process for assessing site conditions, selecting appropriate technologies, and integrating drainage with other landscape elements.

ii. Equipment and Technology

- Another important factor to consider is the contractor's access to and proficiency with the latest equipment and technology for drainage projects. Look for contractors who invest in state-of-the-art tools, machinery, and software to enhance the efficiency, precision, and quality of their work.
- Ask about their use of technologies such as GPS surveying, 3D modeling, or drone imaging for site analysis and design, as well as their equipment fleet for excavation, trenching, and installation. Contractors with advanced equipment and technology may be able to complete projects faster, more accurately, and with less disruption to your landscape.

iii. Subcontracting and Collaboration
- Depending on the complexity and scope of your drainage project, your contractor may need to subcontract or collaborate with other professionals, such as engineers, surveyors, or landscapers. Ask about their experience and approach to subcontracting and collaboration, including how they select and manage subcontractors, and how they ensure seamless communication and coordination among all parties.
- Look for contractors who have established relationships with reputable and qualified subcontractors, and who are transparent and proactive about their subcontracting practices. A contractor who can effectively leverage the expertise and resources of other professionals may be better equipped to handle complex or multi-faceted drainage projects.

d. **Professionalism and Communication**
i. Responsiveness and Punctuality
- When working with a drainage contractor, clear and timely communication is essential for keeping your project on track and avoiding misunderstandings or delays. From your initial inquiry to the final walkthrough, pay attention to how responsive and punctual the contractor is in their interactions with you.
- Look for contractors who return your calls or emails promptly, show up on time for appointments, and keep you informed of any changes or updates to the project schedule or scope. A contractor who is reliable and communicative from the start is more likely to maintain that level of professionalism throughout the project.

ii. Listening and Understanding
- Another key aspect of professionalism is the contractor's ability to listen to and understand your needs, preferences, and concerns. During your initial consultation or proposal review, observe how well the contractor pays attention to your input and feedback, and how they incorporate that information into their recommendations and plans.
- Look for contractors who ask thoughtful questions, provide clear and thorough explanations, and seek to align their expertise with your vision and goals for the project. A contractor who genuinely listens and understands your perspective is more likely to deliver a solution that meets or exceeds your expectations.

iii. Contracts and Documentation
- Finally, consider the contractor's approach to contracts and documentation. A professional contractor should provide a detailed and transparent contract that clearly outlines the scope of work, timeline, payment terms, and any contingencies or warranties.
- Look for contracts that are easy to understand, free of ambiguous or vague language, and fair and reasonable in their terms and conditions. Also, ask about the contractor's process for documenting progress, changes, or issues throughout the project, such as daily logs, photos, or reports.

By following these criteria and best practices for choosing the right contractor for your yard drainage project, you can minimize the risks and maximize the rewards of your investment. While it may take some time and effort to research and compare different contractors, the payoff in terms of quality, value, and peace of mind is well worth it. Remember, a successful drainage project is not just about the final product, but also about the process and the partnership behind it. By choosing a contractor who is qualified, experienced, professional, and responsive, you can ensure a smoother, more satisfying, and more sustainable outcome for your yard and your home.

Questions to Ask Before Hiring a Professional

When considering hiring a professional for your yard drainage project, it's essential to ask the right questions to ensure that you're making an informed and confident decision. Beyond the basic criteria of qualifications, experience, and professionalism, there are several specific questions you should ask to gauge the contractor's suitability, reliability, and compatibility with your needs and expectations. In this section, we'll provide a detailed list of questions to ask before hiring a drainage professional, along with explanations of why each question is important and what to look for in the answers.

a. Project Scope and Approach

i. What is your process for assessing and diagnosing drainage issues?

- This question helps you understand how thorough and systematic the contractor is in their approach to identifying and analyzing drainage problems. Look for answers that demonstrate a comprehensive and data-driven process, such as site surveys, soil tests, hydrologic modeling, or root cause analysis.
- A contractor who takes a holistic and evidence-based approach to assessment is more likely to identify the underlying causes and appropriate solutions for your drainage issues, rather than just treating the symptoms or applying a one-size-fits-all approach.

ii. What are your recommendations for solving my specific drainage problems, and why?
- This question allows you to evaluate the contractor's expertise, creativity, and communication skills in proposing and explaining drainage solutions. Look for answers that are clear, specific, and well-reasoned, with a logical connection between the identified problems and the recommended solutions.
- A contractor who can articulate the benefits, drawbacks, and trade-offs of different options, and who can adapt their recommendations to your specific site conditions, budget, and preferences, is more likely to deliver a customized and effective solution for your needs.

iii. How do you integrate drainage solutions with other landscape elements and features?
- This question helps you assess the contractor's ability to think holistically and collaboratively about drainage in the context of your larger landscape and property. Look for answers that demonstrate an understanding of how drainage interacts with and impacts other aspects of your yard, such as grading, plantings, hardscapes, or irrigation.
- A contractor who can seamlessly integrate drainage solutions with your existing or planned landscape features, and who can optimize the aesthetic, functional, and ecological value of your yard as a whole, is more likely to deliver a cohesive and sustainable outcome.

b. Project Timeline and Logistics

i. What is your estimated timeline for completing the project, and what factors could impact that timeline?

- This question helps you set realistic expectations and plan accordingly for the duration and phasing of your drainage project. Look for answers that provide a clear and detailed breakdown of the project timeline, including key milestones, dependencies, and contingencies.
- A contractor who is transparent and proactive about communicating the timeline, and who has a track record of meeting deadlines and managing delays or changes effectively, is more likely to keep your project on schedule and minimize disruptions to your daily life.

ii. What are your policies and procedures for managing subcontractors, permits, and inspections?

- This question helps you understand how the contractor handles the logistical and regulatory aspects of your drainage project, and how they ensure quality control and compliance throughout the process. Look for answers that demonstrate a systematic and responsible approach to subcontracting, permitting, and inspections.
- A contractor who has established relationships with reputable and qualified subcontractors, and who is familiar with and adherent to the relevant codes, standards, and best practices for drainage work, is more likely to execute your project smoothly and legally.

iii. What should I expect in terms of communication, updates, and decision-making during the project?
- This question sets the stage for a clear and productive working relationship with your contractor, and helps you understand their communication style, frequency, and channels. Look for answers that emphasize regular, transparent, and accessible communication, with a clear process for providing updates, addressing concerns, and making decisions collaboratively.
- A contractor who values open and responsive communication, and who has a system in place for keeping you informed and involved throughout the project, is more likely to foster a positive and successful partnership.

c. **Pricing and Payment**
i. Can you provide a detailed breakdown of your pricing, including materials, labor, and any additional fees or contingencies?
- This question helps you understand the full scope and cost of your drainage project, and allows you to compare pricing and value across different contractors. Look for answers that provide a clear, itemized, and comprehensive breakdown of all costs, with no hidden or vague fees.
- A contractor who is transparent and upfront about their pricing, and who can explain the rationale and competitiveness of their rates, is more likely to be fair and reasonable in their billing practices.

ii. What is your payment schedule and process, and what options do you offer for financing or phasing the project?
- This question helps you plan and budget for the financial aspects of your drainage project, and ensures that you and your contractor are aligned on the payment terms and methods. Look for answers that provide a clear and manageable payment schedule, with options for financing, staging, or adjusting the scope or timeline of the project if needed.
- A contractor who is flexible and accommodating with their payment policies, and who offers a range of options to fit your financial situation and preferences, is more likely to be a good fit for your project and your budget.

iii. What warranties or guarantees do you offer for your work, and what is your process for addressing any issues or defects after the project is completed?
- This question helps you understand the level of confidence and accountability your contractor has in their work, and what recourse you have if something goes wrong or fails to meet your expectations. Look for answers that provide clear, comprehensive, and enforceable warranties or guarantees for the materials, installation, and performance of your drainage system.
- A contractor who stands behind their work with strong warranties and responsive customer service, and who has a proven track record of honoring their commitments and resolving any issues promptly and fairly, is more likely to deliver a quality and lasting solution for your drainage needs.

d. References and Portfolio

i. Can you provide references or testimonials from past clients who have had similar drainage projects completed by your company?

- This question allows you to verify the contractor's experience, reputation, and customer satisfaction through the firsthand accounts of their previous clients. Look for references that are relevant, recent, and willing to share detailed and specific feedback about their experience working with the contractor.
- A contractor who readily provides multiple, positive, and credible references, and who encourages you to contact them directly, is more likely to have a track record of delivering successful and satisfying drainage projects.

ii. Do you have a portfolio of completed drainage projects that I can review, and can you walk me through a few examples that are similar to my project?

- This question gives you a tangible and visual sense of the contractor's capabilities, style, and quality of work, and allows you to see how they have approached and solved drainage problems similar to yours in the past. Look for a portfolio that showcases a diverse range of projects, with clear and informative descriptions, photos, and case studies.
- A contractor who has a comprehensive and impressive portfolio, and who can articulate the unique challenges, solutions, and outcomes of each project, is more likely to have the expertise and creativity to handle your specific drainage needs effectively.

iii. Are you willing to provide a list of suppliers, subcontractors, or other references who can attest to your professionalism, reliability, and quality of work?
- This question allows you to gain a more complete and objective picture of the contractor's reputation and relationships within the industry, beyond just their direct clients. Look for a contractor who is willing to provide references from a variety of sources, such as suppliers, subcontractors, or industry peers, and who has positive and consistent feedback across all references.
- A contractor who has strong and longstanding relationships with reputable suppliers and partners, and who is respected and recommended by others in the field, is more likely to be a reliable and trustworthy choice for your drainage project.

By asking these questions and carefully evaluating the answers, you can gain a deeper understanding of the contractor's qualifications, approach, and fit for your specific drainage project. While no single question or answer will necessarily make or break your decision, the cumulative insights and impressions you gather through this process can help you make a more informed and confident choice. Remember, the goal is not just to find a contractor who can complete your project, but one who can do so in a way that aligns with your values, priorities, and expectations. By taking the time to ask the right questions and listen carefully to the responses, you can set the stage for a successful and rewarding partnership with your drainage professional.

Working with Landscapers and Drainage Specialists

When it comes to designing, installing, and maintaining effective yard drainage systems, working with experienced and knowledgeable professionals can make all the difference. Landscapers and drainage specialists bring a wealth of expertise, resources, and tools to the table, and can help you navigate the complex and often confusing world of drainage solutions with confidence and clarity. However, to get the most value and satisfaction out of these partnerships, it's important to understand the roles, responsibilities, and best practices for working with these professionals. In this section, we'll provide a detailed guide on how to work effectively with landscapers and drainage specialists, from initial consultation to final installation and beyond.

a. Understanding the Roles and Expertise of Landscapers and Drainage Specialists

i. Landscapers

- Landscapers are professionals who specialize in the design, installation, and maintenance of outdoor spaces, including plants, hardscapes, and water features. While not all landscapers have specific expertise in drainage, many have a general understanding of how drainage impacts and interacts with other landscape elements.
- When working with a landscaper on a drainage project, it's important to clarify their experience and capabilities in this area, and to ensure that they are collaborating closely with a drainage specialist or engineer if needed. Landscapers can bring valuable insights and creativity to the aesthetic and functional integration of drainage solutions with your overall landscape design.

ii. Drainage Specialists
- Drainage specialists are professionals who have specific expertise and training in the design, installation, and maintenance of drainage systems, including french drains, catch basins, dry wells, and other solutions. They may have backgrounds in engineering, hydrology, or soil science, and may hold certifications or licenses in drainage-related fields.
- When working with a drainage specialist, it's important to provide them with detailed information about your site conditions, drainage issues, and goals, and to give them the autonomy and resources they need to develop and implement effective solutions. Drainage specialists can bring a data-driven and systematic approach to diagnosing and solving complex drainage problems.

iii. Collaboration and Communication
- In many cases, the most effective approach to yard drainage projects is a collaborative one, where landscapers and drainage specialists work together to integrate their respective expertise and perspectives. This can lead to more holistic, sustainable, and aesthetically pleasing solutions that address both the functional and visual aspects of drainage.
- To facilitate effective collaboration and communication between landscapers and drainage specialists, it's important to establish clear roles, expectations, and channels for sharing information and making decisions. This may involve regular meetings, shared documentation, or designated points of contact to ensure that everyone is aligned and informed throughout the project.

b. Setting Goals and Expectations for Your Drainage Project

i. Defining Your Drainage Needs and Priorities

- Before engaging with a landscaper or drainage specialist, it's important to have a clear understanding of your own drainage needs, issues, and priorities. This may involve conducting a self-assessment of your yard, documenting any visible signs of drainage problems, and identifying any specific areas or features that you want to address.
- It can also be helpful to prioritize your drainage goals in terms of urgency, impact, and budget, so that you can communicate them effectively to your professional partners. For example, you may prioritize fixing a severe erosion issue near your foundation over installing a decorative dry creek bed in a less critical area.

ii. Communicating Your Vision and Preferences

- In addition to your functional drainage needs, it's important to communicate your aesthetic vision and preferences to your landscaper and drainage specialist. This may include your desired style, materials, colors, and overall look and feel of your yard, as well as any specific features or elements that you want to incorporate or avoid.
- By sharing your vision and preferences upfront, you can help your professional partners develop drainage solutions that not only work effectively, but also align with your personal taste and enhance the beauty and value of your property. It can be helpful to provide examples, photos, or sketches to illustrate your ideas and inspire creative solutions.

iii. Establishing a Budget and Timeline
- Another critical aspect of setting expectations for your drainage project is establishing a realistic budget and timeline. This involves considering the scope, complexity, and materials of your desired drainage solutions, as well as any additional costs for permits, inspections, or upgrades.
- It's important to have an open and honest conversation with your landscaper and drainage specialist about your budget constraints and priorities, and to work collaboratively to develop a phased or scaled approach if needed. It's also important to build in some flexibility and contingency into your timeline to account for weather, delays, or unexpected issues that may arise.

c. Collaborating on Design and Planning
i. Site Analysis and Assessment
- One of the first steps in collaborating with a landscaper and drainage specialist is conducting a thorough site analysis and assessment. This typically involves a site visit and walkthrough, where the professionals can observe and document the existing conditions, grades, soils, vegetation, and drainage patterns of your yard.
- During this process, it's important to share any relevant information or history about your property, such as previous drainage issues, repairs, or modifications, as well as any future plans or changes that may impact drainage. It can also be helpful to provide any available maps, surveys, or plans of your property to aid in the analysis and design process.

ii. Concept Development and Refinement
- Based on the site analysis and assessment, your landscaper and drainage specialist will typically develop one or more conceptual designs for your drainage solution. These may include sketches, diagrams, or 3D models that illustrate the proposed layout, features, and materials of your drainage system.
- During the concept development phase, it's important to provide feedback and input on the proposed designs, and to ask questions or raise concerns about any aspects that you don't understand or agree with. It's also important to consider how the proposed drainage solutions will interact with and impact other elements of your landscape, such as plantings, hardscapes, or outdoor living areas.

iii. Material and Product Selection
- Another key aspect of collaboration on design and planning is the selection of materials and products for your drainage system. This may include the type and size of drainage pipes, catch basins, or dry wells, as well as the type and color of decorative elements like grates, covers, or borders.
- Your landscaper and drainage specialist can provide guidance and recommendations on the best materials and products for your specific site conditions, budget, and aesthetic preferences. It's important to consider factors like durability, maintenance, and sustainability when making these selections, as well as any local codes or regulations that may apply.

d. Coordination and Communication During Installation
i. Pre-Construction Meeting and Preparation
- Before breaking ground on your drainage project, it's important to have a pre-construction meeting with your landscaper, drainage specialist, and any other relevant parties, such as subcontractors or inspectors. This meeting can serve to review the final plans, timeline, and logistics of the project, as well as to address any last-minute questions or concerns.
- During this meeting, it's also important to discuss and plan for any necessary preparations, such as utility locates, permits, or site protection measures. It can be helpful to create a checklist or schedule of tasks and responsibilities to ensure that everyone is on the same page and ready to proceed with the installation.

ii. Progress Updates and Quality Control
- Throughout the installation process, it's important to maintain regular communication and coordination with your landscaper and drainage specialist to ensure that the project is progressing smoothly and according to plan. This may involve scheduled progress updates, site visits, or informal check-ins to review the work completed and discuss any issues or changes that arise.
- It's also important to have a system in place for quality control and inspection, to ensure that the installation is meeting the design specifications and performance standards. This may involve third-party testing, documentation, or sign-offs at key milestones or completion points.

iii. Troubleshooting and Adaptability
- Even with the best planning and coordination, unexpected issues or challenges may arise during the installation of your drainage system. These may include unforeseen site conditions, weather delays, material shortages, or design changes necessitated by new information or requirements.
- When these situations occur, it's important to have open and proactive communication with your landscaper and drainage specialist to identify and evaluate potential solutions. This may require flexibility, creativity, and collaboration to adapt the design or installation approach while still meeting the overall goals and objectives of the project.

e. Post-Installation Maintenance and Follow-Up
i. Final Walkthrough and Inspection
- Once the installation of your drainage system is complete, it's important to conduct a final walkthrough and inspection with your landscaper and drainage specialist. This is an opportunity to review the completed work, test the functionality and performance of the system, and identify any punch list items or corrections that need to be addressed.
- During the final walkthrough, it's also important to discuss and document any maintenance requirements, warranties, or recommendations for ongoing care and monitoring of your drainage system. This may include guidance on cleaning, repairs, or seasonal adjustments to ensure optimal performance and longevity.

ii. Maintenance Planning and Education
- To ensure the long-term effectiveness and durability of your drainage system, it's important to develop and implement a regular maintenance plan. This may include tasks like clearing debris from catch basins, flushing pipes, or repairing erosion control measures, as well as monitoring the system for any signs of damage, clogging, or failure.
- Your landscaper and drainage specialist can provide valuable education and guidance on the proper maintenance and care of your specific drainage solutions, as well as any tools, products, or services that can help simplify and streamline the process. It can be helpful to create a written maintenance plan or schedule, with clear instructions and contact information for any professional support needed.

iii. Ongoing Communication and Support
- Even after the installation and initial maintenance period, it's important to maintain open and ongoing communication with your landscaper and drainage specialist for any questions, concerns, or issues that may arise. This may include seasonal check-ins, updated recommendations, or troubleshooting assistance for any performance or aesthetic issues.
- It can also be valuable to continue the collaborative relationship with your professional partners for any future landscaping or drainage projects, as they will have a deep understanding of your site, preferences, and goals. Building a long-term partnership with trusted and responsive professionals can provide peace of mind and added value for your property and your enjoyment of your outdoor spaces.

By following these strategies and best practices for working with landscapers and drainage specialists, you can maximize the benefits and minimize the stress of your yard drainage project. Remember, effective collaboration and communication are key to achieving optimal results and satisfaction, and investing in professional expertise and support can pay off in the long run for the health, beauty, and functionality of your landscape. With the right partners and approach, you can transform your yard drainage challenges into opportunities for enhancement and enjoyment, and create a more sustainable and resilient outdoor environment for years to come.

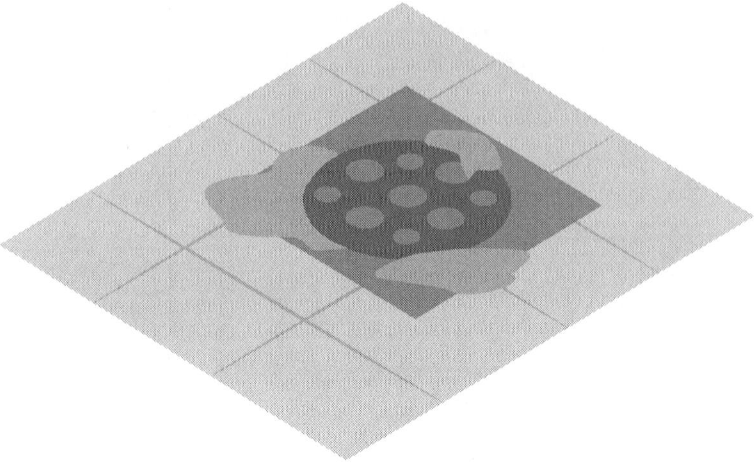

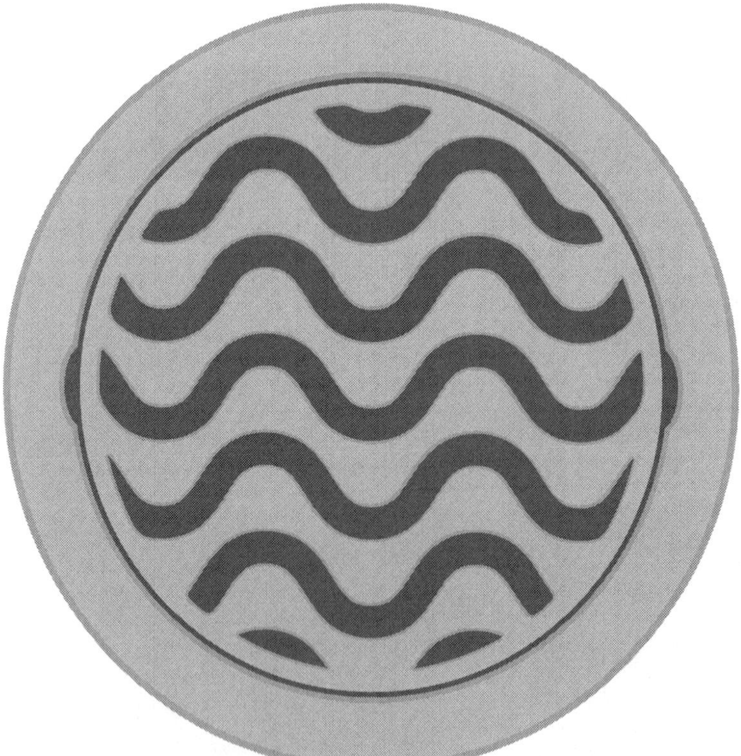

Chapter 7
Case Studies and Success Stories
Real-Life Examples of Effective Yard Drainage Solutions

Case studies and success stories provide valuable insights and inspiration for homeowners facing yard drainage challenges. By examining real-life examples of effective solutions, we can learn from the experiences of others and gain a better understanding of the strategies, techniques, and benefits of properly designed and implemented drainage systems. In this section, we'll explore several case studies of successful yard drainage projects, highlighting the specific problems, solutions, and outcomes of each example.

a. **Case Study 1: Solving Soggy Yard and Foundation Issues with French Drains**
  i. Problem
- A homeowner in a suburb of Chicago had been dealing with a persistently soggy yard and water seepage in their basement for years. The property had heavy clay soil and a relatively flat grade, which prevented water from draining properly and caused it to pool around the foundation and in low-lying areas of the lawn.
- The homeowner had tried various DIY solutions, such as extending downspouts and regrading the soil, but the problems persisted and worsened over time, leading to mold growth, foundation cracks, and unsightly mud patches in the yard.

ii. Solution
- After consulting with a local drainage specialist, the homeowner opted to install a system of French drains to capture and redirect the excess water away from the house and yard. The specialist designed a network of perforated pipes and gravel trenches that would intercept the water at key points and channel it to a safe discharge location.
- The French drain system included a perimeter drain around the foundation, as well as several lateral drains extending out into the yard to address the low-lying areas. The specialist also recommended installing a sump pump in the basement to handle any residual seepage and prevent future moisture issues.

iii. Outcome
- After the French drain system was installed, the homeowner noticed an immediate improvement in the yard and basement conditions. The soil began to dry out and firm up, allowing for healthier grass growth and easier maintenance. The basement remained dry and free of mold, even during heavy rain events.
- The homeowner also appreciated the unobtrusive design of the French drains, which were barely visible on the surface and blended seamlessly with the landscaping. The specialist provided guidance on proper maintenance and care of the system, such as periodic flushing and inspection, to ensure its long-term effectiveness.

iv. Lessons Learned
- This case study illustrates the importance of addressing drainage issues at their root cause, rather than relying on temporary or superficial fixes. By investing in a comprehensive and professionally designed French drain system, the homeowner was able to solve their soggy yard and foundation problems for good.
- It also highlights the value of working with a knowledgeable and experienced drainage specialist who can assess the specific site conditions and recommend tailored solutions. The specialist's expertise in soil types, grading, and drainage techniques ensured that the system was optimized for the homeowner's unique needs and goals.

b. Case Study 2: Mitigating Erosion and Runoff with Bioswales and Rain Gardens

i. Problem
- A homeowner in Seattle had a steeply sloped backyard that was prone to erosion and runoff during the rainy season. The water would flow down the slope and collect at the base of the yard, causing damage to the landscaping and the neighbor's property below.
- The homeowner was concerned about the environmental impact of the runoff, as well as the potential for liability and fines from the city for violating stormwater regulations. They wanted a solution that would not only mitigate the erosion and runoff but also enhance the aesthetic and ecological value of their yard.

ii. Solution
- The homeowner hired a landscape designer who specialized in sustainable stormwater management techniques, such as bioswales and rain gardens. The designer proposed a series of terraced bioswales along the slope, with native plantings and check dams to slow down and filter the runoff.
- At the base of the slope, the designer incorporated a large rain garden that would collect and infiltrate the remaining runoff, while providing a beautiful and biodiverse habitat for pollinators and other beneficial species. The designer also recommended using permeable pavers for the patio area to allow for additional infiltration.

iii. Outcome
- The bioswales and rain garden system effectively mitigated the erosion and runoff issues in the yard, while also creating a stunning and eco-friendly landscape. The terraces and plantings helped to stabilize the slope and prevent soil loss, while the rain garden absorbed and filtered the runoff before it could reach the neighbor's property.
- The homeowner enjoyed the added benefits of the system, such as the increased biodiversity and visual interest of the native plantings, as well as the reduction in their water bill from the decreased need for irrigation. They also received positive feedback from the city and their neighbors for their proactive and responsible approach to stormwater management.

iv. Lessons Learned
- This case study demonstrates the potential for integrating drainage solutions with sustainable landscaping practices, such as bioswales and rain gardens. By working with a designer who understood the principles of green infrastructure, the homeowner was able to achieve multiple goals simultaneously, from erosion control to habitat creation.
- It also showcases the importance of considering the broader environmental and social context of yard drainage, beyond just the immediate property boundaries. By taking a proactive and holistic approach to stormwater management, the homeowner was able to contribute to the health and resilience of their local watershed and community.

c. Case Study 3: Resolving Driveway Flooding and Ice Hazards with Permeable Pavers

i. Problem
- A homeowner in New England had a long, sloped driveway that was prone to flooding and ice accumulation during the winter months. The driveway was paved with traditional asphalt, which was cracked and deteriorated from years of freeze-thaw cycles and heavy use.
- The flooding and ice posed safety hazards for the homeowner and their visitors, as well as damage to their vehicles and the adjacent landscaping. The homeowner had tried various deicing and drainage methods, but none had provided a long-term or sustainable solution.

ii. Solution
- The homeowner consulted with a hardscaping contractor who recommended replacing the asphalt driveway with permeable pavers. The contractor designed a system of interlocking concrete pavers with gaps that would allow water to infiltrate into a gravel base below, instead of running off the surface.
- The contractor also incorporated a series of subsurface drains and a dry well at the bottom of the driveway to handle any excess water that might accumulate during heavy rain or snowmelt events. The permeable paver system was designed to withstand the weight and traffic of vehicles, as well as the freeze-thaw cycles of the local climate.

iii. Outcome
- The permeable paver driveway successfully resolved the flooding and ice issues, while also enhancing the curb appeal and functionality of the property. The homeowner no longer had to worry about slippery surfaces or standing water on their driveway, even during the harshest winter conditions.
- The paver system also helped to reduce the homeowner's environmental impact by allowing for groundwater recharge and filtering out pollutants from the runoff. The dry well and subsurface drains ensured that any excess water was safely and efficiently managed, without impacting the surrounding landscaping or structures.

iv. Lessons Learned
- This case study highlights the versatility and effectiveness of permeable pavers as a drainage solution for driveways and other hardscaped areas. By allowing water to infiltrate through the surface, permeable pavers can mitigate flooding, ice, and runoff issues, while also providing a durable and attractive alternative to traditional paving materials.
- It also demonstrates the value of working with a knowledgeable and experienced hardscaping contractor who can design and install a permeable paver system that is tailored to the specific site conditions and performance requirements. The contractor's expertise in drainage, materials, and construction ensured that the system was optimized for the homeowner's climate, traffic, and aesthetic needs.

These case studies provide just a few examples of the many ways that effective yard drainage solutions can transform problem areas into functional, beautiful, and sustainable landscapes. By learning from the experiences and innovations of others, homeowners can gain the knowledge, confidence, and inspiration they need to tackle their own drainage challenges and achieve their yard goals. Whether through French drains, bioswales, permeable pavers, or other techniques, there are proven strategies and solutions available for every type of drainage issue and site condition. The key is to work with skilled and creative professionals who can help homeowners navigate the options and implement the best approach for their unique needs and context.

Before and After Transformations

Before and after transformations are a powerful way to showcase the dramatic impact that effective yard drainage solutions can have on the appearance, functionality, and value of a property. By comparing the conditions and challenges of a yard before and after a drainage project, we can appreciate the full scope of the improvements and the benefits that homeowners can enjoy as a result. In this section, we'll explore several examples of before and after transformations, highlighting the specific problems, solutions, and outcomes of each project.

a. Transformation 1: From Muddy Mess to Lush Lawn
  i. Before
- A homeowner in a suburb of Houston had a backyard that was constantly muddy and saturated, due to poor grading and clay soil that prevented proper drainage. The yard was unusable for much of the year, with standing water, mosquito breeding, and dead grass patches.
- The homeowner had tried various quick fixes, such as filling in low spots with topsoil and installing a cheap plastic drainage pipe, but these measures only provided temporary relief and often made the problems worse by disturbing the soil structure and creating blockages.

  ii. After
- The homeowner hired a landscape contractor who specialized in drainage and grading solutions. The contractor performed a comprehensive site analysis and proposed a multi-faceted approach to address the root causes of the drainage issues.

- The project involved regrading the entire yard to create a gentle slope away from the house and towards a new swale and dry creek bed feature along the property line. The contractor also installed a system of catch basins and underground pipes to collect and convey the water to a safe discharge point.
- To improve the soil quality and promote better infiltration, the contractor incorporated organic matter and sand into the existing clay soil, and topped the yard with a layer of high-quality topsoil and sod. The contractor also selected moisture-tolerant grass and plant species that could thrive in the improved conditions.

iii. Transformation

- The transformation of the yard was remarkable, with the muddy mess replaced by a lush and vibrant lawn that could be enjoyed year-round. The swale and dry creek bed added visual interest and texture to the landscape, while also providing a functional and attractive drainage feature.
- The homeowner was thrilled with the results and the newfound ability to use their backyard for entertaining, playing, and relaxing. They also appreciated the increased property value and curb appeal that the drainage and landscaping improvements provided.

iv. Lesson

This transformation illustrates the importance of addressing drainage issues holistically and systematically, rather than relying on piecemeal or superficial solutions. By investing in professional analysis, design, and installation, homeowners can achieve lasting and impactful results that enhance both the form and function of their yards.

b. Transformation 2: From Flooded Basement to Dry and Usable Space

i. Before
- A homeowner in a historic neighborhood of Cincinnati had a chronic problem with water intrusion in their basement, due to aging and inadequate foundation drainage systems. The basement would flood during heavy rain events, causing damage to stored items, appliances, and the building structure itself.
- The homeowner had tried various interior waterproofing methods, such as sealants, coatings, and dehumidifiers, but these measures only addressed the symptoms and not the underlying causes of the water intrusion. They were also costly and required frequent maintenance and replacement.

ii. After
- The homeowner consulted with a basement waterproofing specialist who recommended a comprehensive exterior drainage solution to intercept and divert the water before it could reach the foundation. The specialist proposed a system of French drains, footing drains, and a sump pump to collect and remove the water.
- The project involved excavating around the entire perimeter of the foundation, installing a waterproof membrane and drainage board, and backfilling with gravel and soil. The French drains and footing drains were connected to a sump pit and pump in the basement, which discharged the water to a safe location away from the house.

- The specialist also recommended installing gutter guards and downspout extensions to prevent debris buildup and ensure proper water flow away from the foundation. The exterior grading was also adjusted to promote positive drainage and prevent ponding near the house.

iii. Transformation

- The transformation of the basement was dramatic, with the once damp and musty space now dry, clean, and usable for storage, laundry, and even recreational purposes. The homeowner was able to finish the basement with confidence, knowing that the risk of water damage had been effectively mitigated.
- The exterior drainage improvements also had a positive impact on the overall appearance and functionality of the property, with better grading, landscaping, and water management. The homeowner no longer had to worry about flooding or moisture issues, even during the heaviest rain events.

iv. Lesson

- This transformation demonstrates the value of addressing water intrusion issues at their source, rather than relying on interior or cosmetic fixes. By investing in a comprehensive exterior drainage solution, homeowners can protect their basements, foundations, and property from the damaging effects of water infiltration.

c. **Transformation 3: From Eroded Hillside to Terraced Garden Oasis**
  i. Before
  - A homeowner in the Bay Area of California had a steeply sloped backyard that was prone to erosion, landslides, and difficult maintenance. The hillside was bare and unstable, with exposed soil and rocks that would wash away during the rainy season.
  - The homeowner had attempted to stabilize the slope with scattered plantings and makeshift retaining walls, but these measures were insufficient to prevent the ongoing erosion and safety hazards. The yard was also inaccessible and unusable for most of the year.
  ii. After
  - The homeowner hired a landscape architect who specialized in hillside stabilization and sustainable design. The architect proposed a series of terraced gardens and retaining walls to break up the slope and create level planting areas.
  - The project involved grading the hillside into a series of step-like terraces, each supported by a sturdy retaining wall made of natural stone or engineered block. The walls were designed to blend seamlessly with the surrounding landscape and provide visual interest and texture.
  - The terraces were filled with a mix of native and drought-tolerant plants, chosen for their ability to stabilize the soil, provide habitat, and create a lush and colorful tapestry. The architect also incorporated a series of pathways, stairs, and seating areas to make the hillside accessible and enjoyable.

- To manage the water runoff and prevent erosion, the architect designed a system of swales, channels, and infiltration basins that would collect and slow down the water as it flowed down the hillside. The system was integrated with the plantings and hardscape elements to create a cohesive and functional landscape.

iii. Transformation
- The transformation of the hillside was breathtaking, with the once barren and eroded slope now a lush and vibrant garden oasis. The terraces and retaining walls provided structure and stability, while the diverse plantings added color, texture, and life to the landscape.
- The homeowner was overjoyed with the results and the newfound ability to enjoy their backyard as an extension of their living space. They also appreciated the increased safety, sustainability, and biodiversity that the hillside stabilization and landscaping provided.

iv. Lesson
- This transformation showcases the potential for turning drainage challenges into opportunities for creativity, beauty, and functionality. By working with the natural topography and processes of the site, rather than against them, homeowners can achieve stunning and resilient landscapes that manage water wisely and provide multiple benefits.

These before and after transformations provide inspiring examples of the power and potential of effective yard drainage solutions. By seeing the tangible results and impacts of these projects, homeowners can envision the possibilities for their own yards and gain the motivation and confidence to pursue their own transformations. Whether dealing with soggy lawns, flooded basements, or eroded hillsides, there are proven strategies and solutions available to transform problem areas into beautiful, functional, and sustainable landscapes. The key is to work with skilled and creative professionals who can help homeowners realize their vision and achieve their goals, while also addressing the underlying drainage issues and opportunities of the site.

Lessons Learned from Homeowners and Professionals

Designing, installing, and maintaining effective yard drainage solutions can be a complex and challenging process, with many variables and considerations to navigate. However, by learning from the experiences and insights of homeowners and professionals who have successfully tackled drainage projects, we can gain valuable lessons and best practices to inform our own efforts. In this section, we'll explore some of the key lessons learned from homeowners and professionals, based on their real-world successes, challenges, and innovations.

a. Lessons from Homeowners
  i. Invest in Professional Expertise
- One of the most common lessons cited by homeowners who have completed yard drainage projects is the importance of investing in professional expertise. While it may be tempting to try to save money with DIY approaches or cheap quick fixes, these often prove to be more costly and less effective in the long run.
- Homeowners who have hired skilled and experienced professionals, such as landscape architects, drainage contractors, or soil scientists, report better outcomes, fewer headaches, and greater peace of mind. These professionals bring specialized knowledge, tools, and techniques that can help homeowners avoid common pitfalls and achieve optimal results.

- Lesson: Don't skimp on professional expertise when it comes to yard drainage. Investing in qualified and reputable professionals can pay off in terms of better design, installation, and performance, as well as reduced risk and stress.

ii. Plan for the Long Term
- Another key lesson emphasized by homeowners is the importance of planning for the long term when it comes to yard drainage. While it may be tempting to focus on short-term fixes or cosmetic improvements, true success requires a holistic and forward-thinking approach.
- Homeowners who have taken the time to assess their site conditions, understand their drainage needs and goals, and develop a comprehensive and sustainable plan report better long-term outcomes and satisfaction. This may involve phasing projects over time, budgeting for ongoing maintenance and upgrades, and considering the broader environmental and community impacts of their choices.
- Lesson: Take a long-term and holistic perspective when planning yard drainage projects. Consider not just the immediate problems and solutions, but also the future needs, opportunities, and impacts of your choices.

iii. Communicate and Collaborate
- A third lesson highlighted by homeowners is the value of communication and collaboration throughout the yard drainage process. From initial planning and design to installation and maintenance, successful projects require clear and frequent communication among all stakeholders, including homeowners, professionals, contractors, and regulators.

- Homeowners who have prioritized communication and collaboration report better relationships, fewer misunderstandings, and more satisfying results. This may involve setting clear expectations and goals, asking questions and providing feedback, and being open to new ideas and approaches.
- Lesson: Make communication and collaboration a priority in your yard drainage project. Work closely with your team to establish shared goals, navigate challenges, and celebrate successes along the way.

b. Lessons from Professionals
i. Start with a Comprehensive Site Analysis
- One of the most important lessons emphasized by drainage professionals is the need to start with a comprehensive site analysis before designing or installing any solutions. This involves a thorough assessment of the site's topography, soils, hydrology, vegetation, and infrastructure, as well as any relevant codes, regulations, or constraints.
- Professionals who conduct rigorous site analyses report better outcomes, fewer surprises, and more tailored solutions. By understanding the unique characteristics and challenges of each site, professionals can develop drainage strategies that are optimized for the specific context and goals of the project.
- Lesson: Don't skip the site analysis phase of your yard drainage project. Invest time and resources upfront to gather data, assess conditions, and identify opportunities and constraints that will inform your design and installation.

ii. Design for Function and Aesthetics
- Another key lesson stressed by drainage professionals is the importance of designing for both function and aesthetics in yard drainage solutions. While the primary goal of drainage is to manage water effectively and efficiently, the best solutions also enhance the beauty, usability, and value of the landscape.
- Professionals who prioritize both function and aesthetics in their designs report higher client satisfaction, increased property values, and more sustainable outcomes. This may involve integrating drainage features into the overall landscape design, selecting materials and plants that serve multiple purposes, and considering the experiential qualities of the space.
- Lesson: Don't treat yard drainage as a purely utilitarian exercise. Strive to create solutions that are both functional and beautiful, and that contribute to the overall quality and character of the landscape.

iii. Innovate and Adapt
- A final lesson highlighted by drainage professionals is the need for innovation and adaptation in the face of changing conditions and challenges. As climate patterns, development pressures, and regulatory frameworks evolve, professionals must be able to innovate new strategies and technologies to meet the needs of their clients and communities.
- Professionals who embrace innovation and adaptation report more resilient and sustainable outcomes, as well as opportunities for growth and leadership in their field. This may involve experimenting with new materials, techniques, or partnerships, as well as staying current with the latest research and best practices.

- Lesson: Embrace innovation and adaptation as a core value in your yard drainage work. Be open to new ideas and approaches, and seek out opportunities to learn, experiment, and collaborate with others in the field.

These lessons learned from homeowners and professionals provide valuable insights and guidance for anyone embarking on a yard drainage project. By heeding the wisdom and experience of those who have gone before, we can avoid common pitfalls, optimize our efforts, and achieve better outcomes for our landscapes and communities. Whether we are homeowners seeking to improve our own yards, or professionals striving to serve our clients and advance our field, these lessons offer a roadmap for success and sustainability in yard drainage. By investing in expertise, planning for the long term, communicating and collaborating effectively, conducting thorough site analysis, designing for function and aesthetics, and innovating and adapting continuously, we can create yard drainage solutions that are both effective and meaningful, and that contribute to the health, beauty, and resilience of our built and natural environments.

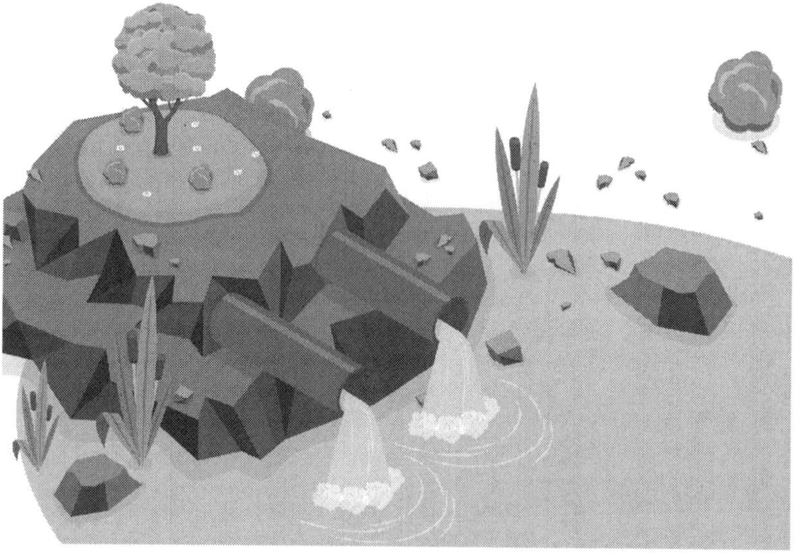

Chapter 8
Resources and Further Reading
Recommended Books and Publications

When it comes to learning about yard drainage solutions and landscaping techniques, there is a wealth of knowledge available in books and publications. These resources offer in-depth information, practical advice, and inspiring case studies that can help homeowners and professionals alike to design, install, and maintain effective drainage systems. In this section, we'll highlight some of the top recommended books and publications for those seeking to expand their understanding and skills in yard drainage.

a. "The Homeowner's Guide to Drainage: Protecting Your Home from Water Damage" by Jaeson R. Swift

- This comprehensive guide is a must-read for any homeowner looking to prevent or mitigate water damage on their property. Swift provides clear and concise explanations of the various types of drainage issues that can affect homes, as well as step-by-step instructions for assessing, designing, and installing effective drainage solutions.
- The book covers a wide range of topics, from grading and gutters to French drains and sump pumps, and includes helpful illustrations, checklists, and resources throughout. Swift also emphasizes the importance of regular maintenance and offers tips for troubleshooting common problems and working with professionals when needed.

- Whether you are a novice or an experienced homeowner, this book offers valuable insights and practical guidance for protecting your home and landscape from the damaging effects of water.

b. "Sustainable Stormwater Management: A Landscape-Driven Approach to Planning and Design" by Thomas W. Liptan and J. David Santen Jr.
- This visually stunning and informative book is a go-to resource for professionals and advanced enthusiasts interested in sustainable stormwater management. Liptan and Santen present a landscape-driven approach to planning and design that integrates natural processes, green infrastructure, and community priorities.
- The book features in-depth case studies, technical details, and best practices for a wide range of sustainable drainage solutions, from rain gardens and bioswales to permeable pavement and green roofs. The authors also explore the social, economic, and environmental benefits of sustainable stormwater management and offer strategies for overcoming common barriers and challenges.
- With its emphasis on interdisciplinary collaboration, adaptive management, and long-term sustainability, this book is an essential reference for anyone seeking to create resilient and regenerative landscapes that manage water wisely and beautifully.

c. "**Rainwater Harvesting for Drylands and Beyond, Volume 1:** Guiding Principles to Welcome Rain into Your Life and Landscape" by Brad Lancaster
- This inspiring and practical book is a classic in the field of rainwater harvesting and sustainable water management. Lancaster draws on his extensive experience and passion for water conservation to present a comprehensive guide to capturing, storing, and using rainwater in arid and semi-arid regions.
- The book covers a wide range of topics, from site assessment and design to installation and maintenance of rainwater harvesting systems. Lancaster emphasizes a holistic and regenerative approach that works with natural processes and integrates multiple benefits, such as soil conservation, habitat creation, and food production.
- With its engaging writing style, helpful illustrations, and practical tips, this book is a valuable resource for anyone looking to create more self-reliant and sustainable landscapes that make the most of precious rainwater resources.

Online Forums and Communities

In addition to books and publications, online forums and communities offer a wealth of knowledge, support, and inspiration for those interested in yard drainage solutions and landscaping techniques. These digital spaces allow homeowners and professionals to connect with others who share their interests, ask questions, share experiences, and learn from a diverse range of perspectives and expertise. In this section, we'll highlight some of the top online forums and communities for yard drainage enthusiasts.

a. Houzz - Drainage Forum
- Houzz is a popular online platform for home design, remodeling, and landscaping, with a dedicated forum for drainage topics. The Drainage Forum is a vibrant community of homeowners, professionals, and experts who share advice, ideas, and experiences related to yard drainage solutions.
- The forum covers a wide range of topics, from basic concepts and terminology to specific products and techniques. Users can ask questions, post photos, and receive feedback and recommendations from others who have tackled similar challenges or projects.
- With its user-friendly interface, active moderation, and wealth of resources, the Houzz Drainage Forum is a great place to start for anyone seeking to learn about or troubleshoot yard drainage issues.

- With its focus on practical solutions, product reviews, and design ideas, the Landscaping Network Drainage Solutions Forum is a great resource for anyone looking to implement effective and attractive yard drainage solutions.

These recommended books, publications, and online forums and communities offer a wealth of knowledge, inspiration, and support for anyone interested in yard drainage solutions and landscaping techniques. By exploring these resources and engaging with the diverse perspectives and expertise they offer, homeowners and professionals can deepen their understanding, expand their skills, and connect with others who share their passion for creating beautiful, functional, and sustainable landscapes that manage water wisely. Whether you are just starting out or looking to take your knowledge to the next level, these resources provide a valuable foundation and ongoing support for your yard drainage journey.

-

Local Resources and Organizations

When it comes to implementing yard drainage solutions and landscaping techniques, it's important to be aware of the local resources and organizations that can provide guidance, support, and expertise specific to your area. These local entities can offer valuable information on regional soil types, climate patterns, native plants, and best practices for managing water in your specific context. They can also connect you with local professionals, suppliers, and community groups who share your interests and can provide targeted advice and assistance. In this section, we'll explore some key local resources and organizations to consider when planning and executing your yard drainage projects.

a. Cooperative Extension Services
- Cooperative Extension Services are local offices affiliated with land-grant universities that provide research-based information and education to farmers, gardeners, and communities. Many Extension offices have horticulture, agriculture, or natural resources experts who can provide guidance on yard drainage, soil health, plant selection, and other landscaping topics.
- Extension offices often offer free or low-cost soil testing services, which can help you determine your soil type, fertility, and drainage characteristics. They may also provide workshops, demonstrations, or site visits to help homeowners and professionals learn about and implement best practices for water management and conservation.

- To find your local Cooperative Extension office, visit the National Institute of Food and Agriculture website and search for your state and county.

b. Soil and Water Conservation Districts
- Soil and Water Conservation Districts (SWCDs) are local government entities that work to protect and conserve soil and water resources in their jurisdictions. SWCDs often provide technical assistance, education, and cost-share programs to help landowners and managers implement conservation practices, including yard drainage solutions.
- SWCDs may offer services such as site assessments, design assistance, and installation guidance for practices such as rain gardens, bioswales, and erosion control measures. They may also have tools, such as soil maps and hydrologic models, that can help you understand your site's drainage characteristics and plan appropriate interventions.
- To find your local SWCD, visit the National Association of Conservation Districts website and use their directory search tool.

c. Master Gardener Programs
- Master Gardener Programs are volunteer programs that train individuals in horticulture and gardening practices, who then share their knowledge with their communities. Master Gardeners often have expertise in plant selection, soil management, and water conservation techniques that can be applied to yard drainage projects.

- Master Gardeners may offer workshops, demonstrations, or one-on-one consultations to help homeowners and professionals learn about and implement best practices for water-wise landscaping. They may also have connections to local plant nurseries, suppliers, and other resources that can support your yard drainage efforts.
- To find a Master Gardener Program near you, contact your local Cooperative Extension office or search online for programs in your state or region.

d. Watershed Organizations and Councils
- Watershed organizations and councils are groups that work to protect and restore the health of local watersheds, which are areas of land that drain to a common waterbody. These groups often have knowledge and expertise in stormwater management, green infrastructure, and other practices that can help mitigate the impacts of development on water resources.
- Watershed organizations may offer education, outreach, and technical assistance programs to help homeowners and professionals implement yard drainage solutions that benefit both individual properties and the larger watershed. They may also have volunteer opportunities, such as stream cleanups or rain garden installations, that can help you learn and contribute to local water conservation efforts.
- To find watershed organizations near you, search online for your local watershed name or contact your state or regional environmental agency for recommendations.

Glossary of Drainage and Landscaping Terms

When learning about and implementing yard drainage solutions and landscaping techniques, it's helpful to have a basic understanding of the terminology and concepts used in these fields. This glossary provides definitions and explanations for some of the most common terms related to drainage and landscaping, organized alphabetically for easy reference.

a. Berm: A raised barrier or mound of soil, often used to direct or control the flow of water in a landscape.
b. Bioretention: A water management practice that uses soil, plants, and microbes to filter and treat stormwater runoff.
c. Bioswale: A vegetated channel or depression designed to slow, filter, and infiltrate stormwater runoff.
d. Catch Basin: A subsurface structure that collects and directs water from surface runoff or underground drains.
e. Culvert: A pipe or channel that allows water to flow under a road, driveway, or other surface.
f. Downspout: A vertical pipe that carries water from a gutter to the ground or a drainage system.
g. Dry Creek Bed: A decorative landscape feature that mimics a natural streambed, often used to direct and infiltrate water.
h. Dry Well: An underground structure that collects and infiltrates stormwater runoff, typically filled with gravel or other porous material.
i. Erosion: The process by which soil or rock is worn away by water, wind, or other forces.

j. French Drain: A trench filled with gravel and a perforated pipe that collects and directs subsurface water away from an area.
k. Grade: The slope or inclination of a surface, often expressed as a percentage or ratio.
l. Hardscape: The non-living elements of a landscape, such as patios, walls, and walkways.
m. Impervious Surface: A surface that does not allow water to pass through, such as concrete or asphalt.
n. Infiltration: The process by which water enters and moves through soil or other porous media.
o. Mulch: A layer of organic or inorganic material applied to the surface of soil to conserve moisture, suppress weeds, and regulate temperature.
p. Permeable Pavement: A type of pavement that allows water to pass through and infiltrate into the underlying soil.
q. Rain Garden: A shallow depression planted with native vegetation that collects and infiltrates stormwater runoff.
r. Retaining Wall: A structure that holds soil in place and prevents erosion on a slope or hillside.
s. Runoff: The portion of precipitation or irrigation water that flows over the surface of the land, rather than infiltrating into the soil.
t. Sump Pump: A mechanical device used to remove water that has accumulated in a sump pit or other low-lying area.
u. Swale: A shallow, vegetated channel or depression designed to convey and infiltrate stormwater runoff.
v. Topography: The physical features and contours of a landscape, such as hills, valleys, and slopes.
w. Transpiration: The process by which plants release water vapor through their leaves and stems.

x. Watershed: An area of land that drains to a common waterbody, such as a river, lake, or ocean.

y. Weep Hole: A small opening in a retaining wall or other structure that allows water to drain and relieve hydrostatic pressure.

z. Xeriscaping: A landscaping approach that emphasizes the use of drought-tolerant plants and efficient irrigation techniques to conserve water.

By familiarizing yourself with these local resources and organizations, as well as the key terms and concepts related to drainage and landscaping, you can build a strong foundation of knowledge and support for your yard drainage projects. Whether you are a homeowner seeking to improve your property's water management, or a professional looking to expand your expertise and network, these resources offer valuable information, guidance, and connections that can help you achieve your goals and create more sustainable, resilient, and beautiful landscapes.

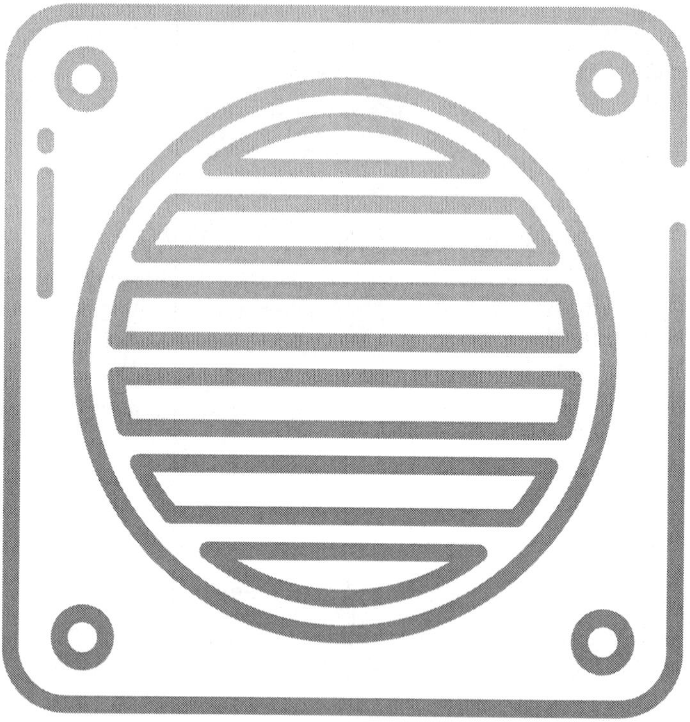

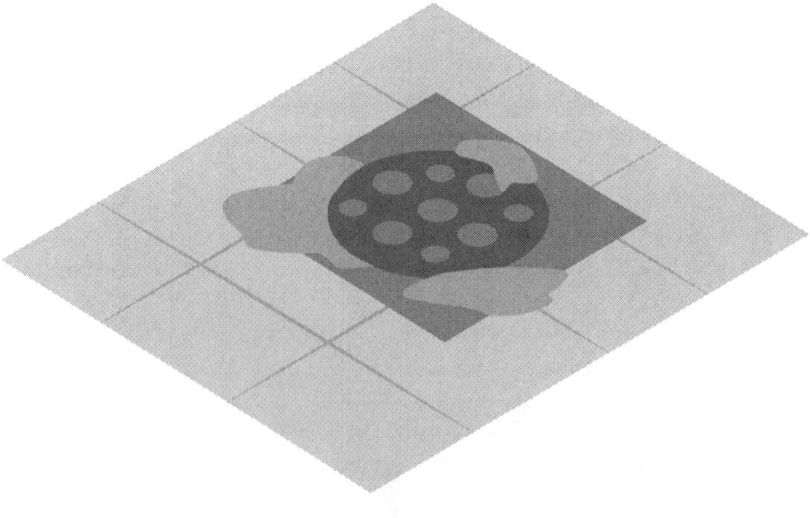

Conclusion

In this comprehensive guide, we have explored the fundamental principles, strategies, and techniques for designing, installing, and maintaining effective yard drainage solutions. From understanding the basic concepts of soil, water, and topography, to selecting and implementing appropriate drainage systems and landscaping practices, we have provided a wealth of knowledge and practical guidance to help homeowners and professionals alike create beautiful, functional, and sustainable landscapes that manage water wisely.

Throughout the book, we have emphasized the importance of a holistic, site-specific, and collaborative approach to yard drainage. By taking the time to assess your unique site conditions, identify your goals and priorities, and engage with skilled and knowledgeable professionals, you can develop customized solutions that address the root causes of drainage issues while enhancing the overall health, beauty, and value of your property.

We have also highlighted the many benefits of investing in effective yard drainage, from preventing water damage and erosion to creating more diverse and resilient ecosystems. By working with natural processes and incorporating green infrastructure techniques, such as rain gardens, bioswales, and permeable pavement, you can not only solve drainage problems but also contribute to the larger goals of water conservation, habitat creation, and community well-being.

The case studies, before-and-after examples, and lessons learned from real-life projects demonstrate the transformative potential of well-designed and executed drainage solutions. From turning muddy messes into lush oases to converting flooded basements into valuable living spaces, these stories inspire us to see the opportunities and possibilities inherent in even the most challenging drainage situations.

As we have seen, creating effective yard drainage is not a one-time fix, but an ongoing process of observation, adaptation, and stewardship. By staying informed about best practices, innovative technologies, and local resources, and by maintaining and upgrading our drainage systems over time, we can ensure their long-term performance and resilience in the face of changing environmental and societal conditions.

Ultimately, the key to success in yard drainage lies in cultivating a sense of curiosity, creativity, and collaboration. By learning from the wisdom of nature, the expertise of professionals, and the experiences of our fellow homeowners and community members, we can develop a deeper understanding and appreciation of the vital role that water plays in our landscapes and our lives.

As you embark on your own yard drainage journey, we hope that this book serves as a valuable resource and companion, guiding you through the challenges and rewards of creating a landscape that works with water, rather than against it.

By embracing the principles and practices of sustainable yard drainage, you can become a steward of your land, a partner in your watershed, and a leader in your community, contributing to a more vibrant, resilient, and regenerative future for all.

Made in the USA
Columbia, SC
12 July 2025